Per La Famiglia

Per La *Famiglia*

Memories and Recipes of Southern Italian Home Cooking

Emily Richards

whitecap

For Matthew, Nicolas and Adriana
to continue making memories
of food with family

Editor: Jordie Yow
Designer: Michelle Furbacher
Food Photographer: Jonathan Bielaski
Food Stylist: Emily Richards
Proofreader: Moira Sanders

Printed in Canada

**Library and Archives Canada Cataloguing
in Publication**

Richards, Emily, author
Per la famiglia : memories and recipes of southern
Italian home cooking / Emily Richards.

ISBN 978-1-77050-224-6 (pbk.)

1. Cooking, Italian--Southern style. 2. Cookbooks.
I. Title.

TX723.2.S65R53 2014   641.5945'7   C2014-903218-8

We acknowledge the financial support of the
Government of Canada, and the Province of British
Columbia through the Book Publishing Tax Credit.

Canadä

21 20 19 18 17 16 15   1 2 3 4 5 6 7

This book was printed on chlorine-free paper and made
with 10% post-consumer waste.

INTRODUCTION

Per La Famiglia simply translated from Italian means "for the family." As a daughter of Italian immigrants, I take that statement to heart in all that I do. When my maternal grandparents, Nonna Ortenzia and Nonno Nicola, came to Canada they had two young daughters. They didn't know the language, but they had family here to help them get on their feet.

When my father came to Canada as a young adult, he was welcomed by his sisters (my future aunts) who were already in Canada. They helped him get started in his new life. It is this support and love for family that has always surrounded me. I am lucky to be part of this family and to share their love of family and food.

Both of my parents are from Southern Italy, Calabria to be exact. The influences of those hot summer days and chilly winter nights have never left them. Walking up mountain tops and jumping into the ocean are distant memories for them now, however, if you ask them about a certain relative or what they ate during a certain festival, memories reappear like it was yesterday. Food and family have that kind of power over people, particularly for immigrants as they venture into a new country and are only able to bring a few things with them as they start a new future.

When learning these stories of time past, I've always asked how a certain recipe was made so that I could replicate it, only to find that the aunt or Nonna who was the expert had not written it down. They had simply reproduced that delicious dish themselves time and again. It was part of a family's legacy to know how to make something your mother had made. Children were welcome in the kitchen and were put to work helping recreate these dishes. It was a necessity if you wanted to preserve these recipes for your own family. And that is what I aim to do with *Per La Famiglia*.

Southern Italy What is considered Southern Italy? Some will say anything south of Rome. When you speak to other Italians, they may not consider Sicily or Sardinia as part of the South as they are islands. I disagree, as they have some of the best cuisine the South has to offer. If you look at the bottom half of Italy's boot, you will find the deliciousness of the regions of Abruzzo, Basilicata, Campania, Puglia, Molise and Calabria.

The south of Italy is special to me and is the direct link to my heritage, as most of my immediate family comes from these regions. Even those that have moved to other countries have a sense of coming home when heading back to the South of Italy. Italians are good at making you feel welcome in their home; open arms and kitchens are what I know and have always gravitated to—and this happens throughout Italy—but I do have a soft spot for Southern Italians, in particular.

The food of the South reflects its climate. The mountainous areas are home to goats; much of the milk that is used for cheese is from goat or sheep. Yet there are still wonderful cow and water buffalo milk cheeses that are produced to make the perfect pizza cheese, mozzarella. There is plenty of sunshine so tomatoes and olives grow abundantly and add to the world supply of tomato sauce, canned tomatoes and olive oil. Many of the dishes from the South are those that everyone is familiar with; dishes that include eggplants, tomatoes, fresh basil and pasta, to name a few.

TO ME, Southern Italian food has always been the simple rustic cuisine that I grew up enjoying. Even with only a few fresh ingredients there was always a delicious dish to put on the table. The prevalence of tomatoes, olive oil, garlic and other fresh local Italian ingredients made it easy to make great food. This does not change when immigrants come to a new country. They used their knowledge from their home country to get digging and start growing food for themselves. They would occasionally be given the luxury of finding out about new wonderful ingredients unavailable to them previously.

There would often be storytelling with my father about those times. He told me about eating nothing but eggs and potatoes because that is all they had. They would only kill a chicken on special occasions because they simply needed the eggs more than the meat. When he came to Canada he said you could go to the store and buy chicken because it wasn't expensive. Things started to change for them because they were now in a new country ready to experience new food.

What a luxury it was in Italy to be surrounded by water in a beautiful country and enjoy fresh fish of all sorts. Moving to a country like Canada, still surrounded by water but much larger, was a bit different. Fish were no longer a regular dinner item until cousins started fishing locally and realized that they still had access to wonderful fish. And so the knowledge began to grow again. As with many immigrants,

curiosity caused them to try new things. Although these immigrants still lived in close proximity to each other to help with language and other necessities, their comfort level in their new home started to increase as the years passed.

The recipes in this book are a snapshot of my life experiences. I could not include all of the recipes, as the list is long. There are many different names for recipes as each dialect of Italy is different. When people of a region use slang to describe a certain food, it tends to stick. In some cases I didn't even know it had another name as I've called it something my whole life. Only in researching this book and talking to many people, I realized others called it something else.

Many unrecorded or traditional recipes have been passed down through generations by family members cooking alongside each other. While sharing these moments, I have taken notes so that the recipes from my own ancestors could be recreated at home.

For example, making homemade pasta alongside an aunt with experience taught me to look for a certain texture in the dough and how to use the pasta machine to achieve the correct size and thickness for different pasta shapes. Being able to feel the dough and understand what the texture is supposed to be brings a new perspective to the recipe. I have tried to be as descriptive as possible with the recipes in this book; sort of a mentor in the kitchen for you.

Sharing time in the kitchen with mothers, aunts and Nonnas is a way to gather your history in the kitchen. By not spending that time in the kitchen with your family members, recipes can be lost. When possible try to get in the kitchen with them and take notes, take part and taste what can become of ingredients. It's a special moment to have.

It was this ongoing learning with family members, started as a young child for me, that helped me gain a love for teaching. I love guiding people to smell, touch and taste so that they can go home and recreate. I believe that if you have experienced the process in person, you can add your own changes and get creative in the kitchen. This book is filled with tales and tips that will make you feel like you are cooking with family, for family.

Dining with Family Food and family go hand in hand. With every celebration or get-together, Italians will have a menu planned out before their guest list. I know I am guilty of that on more than one occasion. As hosts, we want everyone to be happy, to make sure there is enough to eat and that everyone has what they want. This holds true, not just for special occasions but, for weeknight meals, too. I was very spoiled as a child; if I didn't like what was served my Nonna would make me something else. I know parents now cringe at that thought, but I knew she loved me and wanted me to eat. For the record, I always figured out it was last night's leftovers or something from lunch.

My family wasn't rushed when it was time to enjoy food. We sat, ate, drank and chatted about the day's events. And we waited. Yes, if someone didn't show up on time, we would wait until they came home. I loved that. I remember after-school practices could run a bit late but when I got home, my mom, dad and sister would be waiting for me and we would have dinner together. It means so much to have dinner with your family instead of warming up a plate on your own. I continue that tradition with my own family so that we can sit, enjoy a meal together and talk about everyone's day.

This book is truly *per la famiglia*. Not just mine, but yours. There are many great family recipes that don't even exist yet. They should be created and celebrated at your next family get-together or dinner. Start jotting down recipes and notes and cooking with those people that hold the secrets to your family dishes. They may not be willing to cook with you at first, like some of my family members who were concerned I would start making their recipes at family get-togethers instead of them. Once they realised how few people knew these recipes, they saw the importance of letting the next generation taste those delicious flavours and continue their legacy.

Growing up and living in an Italian family has truly been, and continues to be, an

amazing experience. I enjoy my culture and traditions and hope that my children do, too. It is a warm and wonderful feeling to watch them grow and have interest in what is happening with family and food in Italian culture.

I hope that you enjoy many special occasions with your family and friends with delicious food, Italian or not. The recipes in this book represent a love of food and family that I know all cultures have. Sit back and enjoy the stories that unfold in each recipe and celebrate with me and my family. Then step into your kitchen and start having fun. *Mangia con gusto* (eat with enjoyment)!

Wine Many Italian homes include wine with every meal, sometimes even their own wine. This is simply part of Italian culture. Enjoying your food with wine and water has been around for ages, and many a red wine was married to a tomato base sauce or meat, while white was served with fish and lighter dishes. In my house growing up, it was always red, although now my mother shows a strong preference for white, so both are always offered. There is no hard and fast rule, we simply drink what we like. In Italy, wines that are served are usually from the region you are in. Here, we have the opportunity to enjoy wine from many regions and countries so you can enjoy a variety of wines that work deliciously with Italian food.

PER LA FAMIGLIA

Wine is the beverage of choice to serve at any and all gatherings. It originally was to showcase the harvest of grapes that family members had laboured over. We would meticulously prepare the grapes for fermentation in hopes of a perfect glass of ruby red nectar. I recall how after crushing the grapes and leaving them to ferment, the flies would be attracted to what I thought was a vile, stench in our basement. I remember thinking, "How on earth could my family drink this stuff?" It seemed so strong and almost vinegar like, which many of my cousins can attest to. But it wasn't about whether or not it was the best vintage, it was the sense of pride they had that it was homemade wine. No attempt at fancy bottling was done; we would save old glass bottles and fill them with wine and use a marker to write "Vino Rosso" (red wine) on the bottle. Later, as I got older, I noticed that most of those bottles were relabelled "Aceto Rosso" (red vinegar). Some of the best red wine vinegar I've ever had came from those bottles.

Equipment In some of the recipes you will need equipment you may not own such as a pasta machine or pizzelle maker (see bottom right). They are easy to find in cookware shops or Italian stores if you want to use them often. I also include information about other equipment that I use in recipes but have offered up options and methods that could work without any special equipment.

In creating these recipes, I have tried to impart the necessary information to help you recreate it at home.

FOOD GLOSSARY

What I love about Italian food is that you will be able to find everything at most grocery stores. Once you have your pantry stocked you will be ready to get cooking and *mangia bene* (eat well).

Bread Bread is usually served with every Italian meal and antipasti, as well. Bread in our family is very important to eat, but also to make with family members. The path starts with young children playing with the dough. My love of bread started with making the dough with my Nonna.

Fresh yeast bread that is made into loaves or buns can be used for toasting in the morning with breakfast, sliced for sandwiches at lunch and then broken off at the dinner table to dip into leftover pasta sauce. That same bread can be used to make fresh or dry bread crumbs. **Fresh bread crumbs** are made by taking fresh bread and whizzing it around in a food processor. Letting the bread go stale and dry and then grating it or buzzing it in the food processor will give you your own dry bread crumbs.

Something that is also popular in Southern Italian kitchens is using dry bread. This can be enjoyed on its own, stirred into soups or rehydrated with water. **Taralli** are one example, small or large, that are eaten mostly dry.

Taralli are Southern Italian breadsticks that are made from a yeast bread dough that can have spices in them and be sweet or savoury. They vary in size from tiny to very large. **Fresine** is a Southern Italian fresh bread that has been sliced in half and dried at a low heat in an oven to a dry crisp state. It can be enjoyed as is, or more commonly it is run quickly under some water to rehydrate and eaten when fresh bread isn't available.

Cheese Soft or fresh cheeses are used in cooking and baking throughout Italian food. **Ricotta cheese** is a soft textured, mild cheese made traditionally from the whey left behind when making mozzarella or provolone. It has fine, moist granules which make it perfect with pastas or in desserts. Firm ricotta cheese is made the same way as ricotta cheese but more of the water has been removed, making it less spreadable and firmer. **Mascarpone** cheese, which is not used widely in Southern Italy, is a very thick cream that has a very smooth texture. Because of its mild flavour, it can be used in dips, sauces or desserts to add rich texture and taste.

Boconccini is made from fresh **mozzarella** and shaped in small balls of varying sizes that are soft and creamy. They can be enjoyed on their own or in sandwiches, salads and pasta dishes.

The two Italian cheeses I like to use for adding flavour to recipes are **Romano** and **Parmigiano Reggiano** cheese.

Romano cheese is a sheep's milk cheese that tends to be salty and has a strong bite. It is a favourite of the Southern Italians who don't have a lot of cows wandering their mountains. One of the most common versions of Romano cheese is **pecorino,** which is a goat's milk cheese. Used mostly as a grated cheese, it can be added to pasta or even a simple omelette to brighten up the taste considerably. It is also a wonderful addition to pizza, calzones and lasagne.

Real **Parmigiano Reggiano** cheese is imported from the Emilia Romagna Region of Italy, specifically the provinces of Reggio Emilia, Parma, Modena and Bologna. It must be made in Italy to be authentic. You can pick it out from a crowd of cheeses because of the special markings it has on the rind that stamps out Parmigiano Reggiano, a sign of flavour and distinction. Buy a wedge of this to nibble on in chunks or grate fresh over homemade pasta to treat your family.

You can purchase grated **Parmesan** cheeses that are made in Canada and have a rich cheese flavour with a salty bite, like the Italian versions. Keep on the lookout for impostors that don't have to be kept refrigerated as they don't have the great taste and melting quali-

ties of real cheese. Buy fresh Parmesan and buy often.

Grana Padano is another hard cheese that typically is not aged as long as Parmigiano yet can still be eaten in chunks or grated on pastas, salads and vegetables. It has a slightly different texture which makes it less crumbly that other hard cheeses. Grana Padano cheese seems to have a less salty flavour but is richer than some other hard grating cheeses. It also happens to be a little less expensive than Romano or Parmigiano, but that doesn't mean it lacks flavour.

Cured Italian Deli Meats

Finding Italian deli meats is very easy as they are now available presliced in many grocery stores and delis. You can still get them sliced to order which offers up the freshest texture and flavour. Meats like pancetta, prosciutto or dried salami—like sopressata—are all salt-cured meats that sometimes contain hot pepper flakes for heat and pepper sauce or other seasonings for flavour. They are traditionally hung to dry and are humidity and temperature controlled to create the delicate saltiness and texture that Italians love. They are all suitable to be eaten raw, but when they are cooked, the salt and spices come out and the texture changes to become crisp—perfect for salads. There are meats from each region of Italy that are slightly different but that is why there is such a wonderful variety of cured meats.

Capicollo is made from a cut of pork that is a combination of lean meat and fat, mixed with pepper sauce and hot pepper flakes. It is seasoned with salt and then packed in a casing and hung to air dry for 4 months to a 1 year. It is a great addition to an antipasto platter.

Prosciutto is usually made from a leg of pork that is seasoned with pepper sauce and salt and hung to air dry for at least 9 to 18 months. My family makes **prosciuttino** which is the meat of the leg of pork without the bone. We like making this version because it takes less time to age.

Sopressata or sopressa, as some call it, is made from the same meat as Italian sausage with the same balance of fat and meat. It is packed in a larger casing and hung to dry. Some families flatten the sopressata to make a more rectangle shape.

Pancetta is made from pork belly that has been seasoned with spice and pepper sauce to create a mild version or hot pepper flakes are added for a hot version. It is left flat or rolled in a casing to air dry and age. It can be thinly sliced as part of an antipasto plate or used to flavour sauces. It can even be fried until crispy to add to salads.

Mortadella is a large baked ground pork sausage that has small cubes of fat in it. It's thinly sliced and sold as a cold cut in grocery stores and delis. This is a classic Italian luncheon meat that has been served in sandwiches as long as I can remember.

Peppers **Hot pepper flakes** add heat and a little a bit of sweetness to a dish. Whether your container at home says dried chilies, red pepper flakes or hot pepper flakes, these are all the same and will offer the same kick. Typically these are little red chili peppers that have been dried and pulverised to make little flakes that include the whole pepper. They can be added at any stage in a dish, from before it is cooked to after it has finished cooking. When added at the beginning of cooking, they will produce what I like to call a "sweet heat," where it's cooked into the dish you are making. When the hot pepper flakes are added at the end, you will get a more sudden bite of heat in the dish.

Pepperoncini is an Italian word for peppers, typically hot. Pickled pepperoncini are packed in a vinegar brine to give them a zippy tang. They are great on sandwiches and add a kick of flavour to salads, sauces or veggies.

Oils I like to use **extra virgin olive oil** for its rich flavour. I tend to use Southern Italian–style olive oils for their full body and fatty texture, they almost coat your mouth. Northern Italian–style olive oils have more of a fruity, peppery bite to them. Use what you like; taste to see if you enjoy them on their own and if so you will enjoy them in your food. You don't have to break the bank when it comes to olive oil. Buy one that is in your price range and use it often.

Canola oil is another oil I use often, especially for baking and frying. It is flavourless and lets other ingredients shine through. There are also extra virgin canola oils available now that you could use in place of olive oils.

Vegetable oil is a general term for vegetable-based oils including canola oil, sunflower and soybean oils. These oils are also perfect in salad dressings when you don't want the strong flavour of olive oil.

Be sure to store all oils in a cool, dark place, preferably not under the sink where heat from water pipes can steam up a bit. Choose a cupboard or pantry where your oils can be within reach. Most oils now have a best before date, so be sure to use your oil before then. You can check for rancidity by pouring some of the oil out of the bottle and smelling it before use. Do not just smell from the top of the bottle as this is not a reliable method of checking. Purchase the amount of oil you will use within the bottles best before date. If you can finish it in time you do not have to worry about the oil turning rancid. I use lots of oil over the course of a month so my bottles are larger; I never seem to reach the best before date. They do sell smaller bottles so buy the one that suits your needs.

Olives Olives are an important part of Italian cuisine and there are many varieties to choose from.

I can't stop eating yummy **Cerignola olives**. They are big, fat, juicy olives that can be red, black or green. They have a meaty, sweet taste. They are perfect to warm up when made with a spice mixture (see recipe, p. 80). Another type of olive to use is the oil-cured black olives. They are the perfect little snack to serve with drinks or alongside other antipasto favourites.

Oil-cured olives are ripe black olives that are sun or oven-dried so they are a bit wrinkly. They are usually stored in oil and keep their soft texture and salty olive flavour.

Onions and Garlic I like to use local **onions** in my recipes and keep them on hand all the time. Store them in a cool space where they are visible and you can grab them easily when you need them. I most often use regular yellow cooking onions in my recipes but will sometimes specify if I am using a different onion. I also like to keep shallots on hand to change things up but know that you can substitute either in a recipe. **Shallots** are much smaller than onions, for 1 onion, you can substitute 4 shallots.

To help myself out when it comes to **garlic**, I will peel a head or two of garlic and keep it in the fridge so it's easy to grab when I need just a few cloves of garlic. You can keep it in a sealed container in the fridge for a couple of weeks. Make sure it has a tight seal so the rest of your fridge doesn't start smelling like garlic! Use a sharp knife to chop or mince garlic and onions; this will help you keep in all the essential oils that give garlic its great flavour and retain the juices in the onions. The best part of these ingredients is that as they cook, their natural sweetness comes out and adds dimension to a dish.

Parsley I love Italian—or **flat leaf parsley,** as it is also called—for cooking and garnishing dishes. I find that Italian parsley has a clean flavour and works really well with all sorts of cooking, not just Italian. It has a long shelf life in the refrigerator, too. Simply wash it well and pat it dry. Then wrap it in a dry paper towel and store it in the bag you brought it home in or a resealable bag. In your refrigerator's crisper, it can be stored for at least 2 weeks. Be sure to check it when you take it out to use it and remove any dark or mushy leaves. Replace the paper towel when it is wet as the moisture will break down the parsley faster.

Pasta Dried pasta is available in boxes or bags and can be purchased in all grocery stores. There are many brands to choose from so I recommend you try a few and see which one you like the most. You can find short and long pasta that suit your recipe needs.

Short pasta comes in many shapes to suit the sauce of your choice. This pasta is best suited for chunky or meaty sauces. The more common **penne** and **rigatoni** are great for chunky or meaty sauces as the hole in the centre of the pasta catches lots of the sauce inside. Short pasta can have other descriptors on it, like "lisce" which means smooth pasta and "rigate" which means ridged (it has ridges on the outside). Look for fun and interesting shapes that you have not tried before like **scoobi doo** or **cavatappi** (which is shaped like spiral tubes), **wagon wheels** or **rotelle** and **bowtie** or **farfalle** pasta. Many pastas have an English name with one brand and an Italian name with another, so learn them by their shape. You can take a peak at the bag or box and see which one you want to try.

There are many types of long pasta and you can choose thinner or thicker strands of it. The most popular is, of course, **spaghetti.** If you are looking for something thinner, **capellini** or **angel hair** pasta would be a good choice. One of my favourites is **bucatini** which looks like a straw with its thicker diameter and hole in the centre. If you're looking for something long, thin and flat, **linguine** or **fettucini** would be your choice. Be sure to check out some of the more unique long pasta options, too.

Soup pasta is usually very small and is well suited not just for soups, but also salads. They have shapes that children love like **little stars** ("stelline") or **little bowties** ("farfalline"). There are also small strips, squares and ovals, a favourite being **orzo** pasta that can be used to change up a soup, salad or sidedish.

You can make your own **fresh pasta** (see recipe p. 110). It is something that I like getting the whole family involved in. When you make it yourself you can control the thickness of the pasta, giving you great options. You can create your own linguine, lasagne or stuffed pastas once you get started and I've included recipes for using a variety of pasta in this book.

Fresh pasta is also available in grocery stores. It cooks quickly and if you're pressed for time for a **lasagne** and cannot make the pasta you can certainly pick some up. It can be thicker than the homemade version so the texture may be different. It is kept refrigerated and is usually located with all the other fresh pastas and sauces.

Pesto I like keeping pesto in my fridge and using it to add flavour to sauces and vinaigrettes. If you don't have time to make your own pesto, you can buy many good ones in the store. Traditionally, pesto is packed with basil, cheese, garlic, pine nuts and olive oil, but now there are many other varieties to choose from. Look for fresh pesto where fresh pastas are sold. You can also find pesto in jars in the pasta sauce aisle as well. Look for a short ingredient list, with basil being a top ingredient on that list, for the best fresh herb flavour.

Stock Many stocks are used in Italian cooking: chicken, beef, vegetable and fish. When you make your own stock (see recipe p. 22) you can really make your house smell amazing.

Chicken stock has a mild enough flavour that does not take over a dish, but adds more flavour than just water. **Vegetable stock** can be used in place of chicken stock pretty much anytime for a vegetarian option. **Beef stock** is best used with beef but I love using it with veal, pork and lamb to deepen the flavour of dishes. **Fish stock**, while not used in this cookbook, is an excellent addition to fish or seafood risottos and pastas to bring out the fish flavour.

If you don't have time to make your own stocks, here are some store-bought options:

Tetra Paks: This option is ready to go; just shake and pour into a soup or stew and you have a quick and easy meal. They are easy to use to deglaze a pan, but be sure to use it up within the time recommended after you open it. You have the option of low sodium and no salt versions if you want to reduce the salt.

Canned: Canned stock is usually a concentrate of stock that can be diluted with water if it tastes too salty. You can also purchase sodium-reduced versions.

Pastes / Liquids: These are a concentrate of stock flavour that must be diluted with water. These are good to keep in the fridge so you can whip up stock any time. Even for that quick cup of broth to help the sniffles go away.

Cubes: These are concentrated stock flavour that can be diluted in hot water to make stock. Taste them and see which one gives you the most homemade flavour without being too salty. Check the ingredients to see how much natural flavour is added.

Tomatoes I know when late August hits the hunt for the perfect fresh tomatoes starts. Finding those perfect ripe and tasty tomatoes to make sauce or a salad becomes very important. When enjoying tomatoes in a salad, **plum**, **Roma** or **San Marzano** tomatoes work fine but if you want a bit more juiciness and variety of colour, you can look to **round,**

cluster or **heirloom tomatoes**. With a variety of colours and sizes, these tomatoes will offer more interest to your salads and are perfect to add to antipasti as well. **Grape** or **cherry tomatoes** are a wonderful addition to salads and also make a sweet and flavourful sauce to toss with pasta.

As part of an Italian family, canning tomatoes is a big part of our culture and family traditions. For canning tomatoes, I like to use plum tomatoes, Roma or San Marzano tomatoes. They tend to have less seeds and a thicker flesh to provide a wonderful flavour and texture to a tomato sauce.

For many Italians, canning tomatoes is part of their late summer routine. Luckily, in order to enjoy delicious tomatoes year round, you don't have to. Canned tomatoes are often very high quality plum tomatoes that have been picked at the peak of freshness so you have the best flavour for your dishes. If you are making a simple tomato sauce, one tip would be that cooked tomatoes have enough sweetness that you don't need to add sugar or baking soda to the sauce, even if that's a family tradition.

Here is a list of canned tomatoes you will find at the grocery store:

Whole plum or Italian tomatoes: Whole peeled tomatoes with some juice; great to puree or crush for chunky sauces. Adds a rustic feel to recipes.

Diced tomatoes: Tomatoes with juice, cut up into small pieces; great for quick cooking and chunky sauces or stews.

Crushed tomatoes: This is a thick smooth paste of tomatoes; sometimes includes tomato paste as well. Good for thicker sauces, it can be a bit sweeter than other tomatoes.

Stewed tomatoes: These are chunks of tomatoes cooked with onions, peppers and celery, sometimes with other seasonings, such as Italian herbs. These have a slightly different flavour profile but are great to add to chunky soups and sauces.

Tomato paste: This is a concentrated tomato product that can be used to help thicken and intensify the tomato flavour in a recipe. It offers up a bit of sweetness in the dish, too.

Tomato passata: Tomato passata is a strained tomato puree which has no added flavourings and the seeds have been removed. This is great for smooth pasta sauces or to add to soups for a rich tomato broth.

Pasta sauce: You can make your own pasta sauce but sometimes you may have to pick up a jar to help you out. In that case, you may want to buy one that is simple in flavour like tomato and basil. Make sure that tomatoes are the first ingredient in the sauce so that you have primarily a delicious tomato flavour. Use up your pasta sauce once it's opened or if you know you don't need it all, be sure to pack it in an airtight container and freeze it for another use.

FAMILY TREE

Antonio Fernandes   Emilia Assuntina Spina

FERNANDES

Giuseppina "Peppina"   Elena "Lina"   Tommaso

Nicola Fata   Ortenzia Cuglietta

FATA

Giustina   Maria   Amalia "Emily"

FERNANDES

Emily   Tina

James Richards

RICHARDS

Matthew Thomas James   Nicolas Anthony Eston   Adriana Emilia

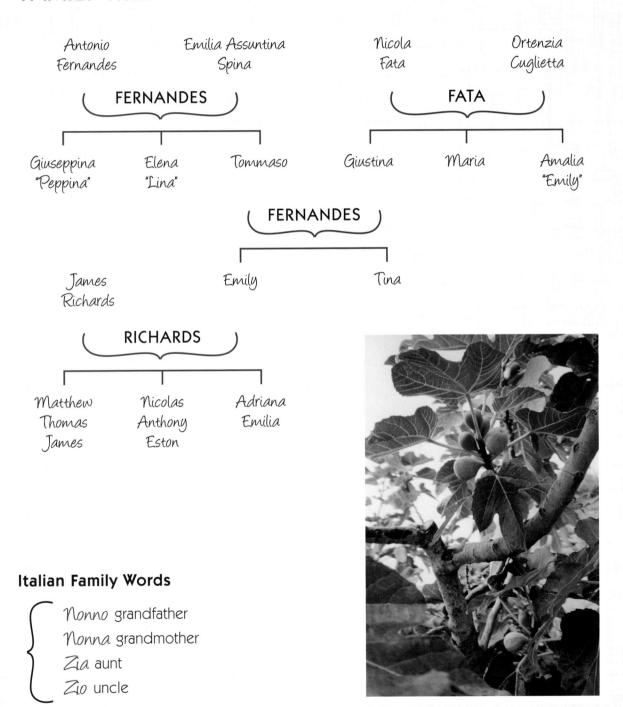

Italian Family Words

- *Nonno* grandfather
- *Nonna* grandmother
- *Zia* aunt
- *Zio* uncle

MENUS FOR ITALIAN CELEBRATIONS

Here are some menus for different Italian celebrations with recipes from throughout the book. We always serve antipasto before the meal, and you can substitute any of your favourites from that chapter. It can be as simple as a dip or crostini or a full antipasto platter with meats and cheeses. At the end of the meal we enjoy fruit and then cap it off with an espresso to help you digest all that delicious food.

St. Joseph's Feast *Festa di San Giuseppe*

Known as Joseph, the spouse of Jesus' mother Mary, he is celebrated on March 19. St. Joseph was said to have saved Southern Italy from the droughts when people prayed to him. He is a name saint as well, so anyone with the name Joseph or Giuseppe or Giuseppine in their name celebrate this special day with wonderful food.

Bread Noodle Soup
Vegetable Pasta
Roasted Sausages

Mixed Green Salad
Cream Filled Doughnuts

Easter *Pasqua*

During *Pasqua*, which is a celebration of spring and the new beginning in the Roman Catholic church calendar, Italian family members gather to celebrate with delicious food.

Spinach Ricotta Cannelloni or
   Ricotta Ball Soup
Balsamic Lamb Chops

Roast Potatoes
Mixed Green Salad
Genetti

Baptism / First Communion / Confirmation
Battesimo / Prima Comunione / La Cresima

Being a Roman Catholic Italian Canadian has led me through various sacraments in the church. Anytime this happens for a family member, we celebrate as a family with food. Sometimes this can be quite a large gathering making it necessary to make some party-size meals. Here is a menu that can be used for any large family get together or special occasion.

Simply Tasty Noodle Soup
Meat Lasagne
Veal Roast with Figs

Roast Potatoes
Tomato Cucumber Salad
Amaretti

Christmas Eve *Vigilia di Natale*

In our family we enjoy *Vigilia di Natale* with a traditional Italian fish and seafood dinner. This is known to many as the "Feast of Seven Fishes." This Southern Italian tradition helps us remember the wait for baby Jesus on Christmas day. There should be no meat in your antipasto this night; enjoy cheese and vegetables though.

Seafood Stuffed Shells
Fried Mixed Fish
Cod with Potatoes and Tomatoes

Cudduri
Ricotta Cannoli

Christmas Day *Natale*

After an evening of fish and seafood the night before, the meat is presented and a full menu of favourites is put on the table. Another gathering of family and friends comes together to be thankful for everything and share delicious food.

Pancetta and Parmesan Pasta
Roast Pork and Potatoes
Garlicky Green Beans

Mixed Green Salad
Panettone Bread Pudding

KITCHEN STAPLES

These are basic recipes that you can keep on hand in the kitchen. I like to make these on the weekend or when I have some extra time so I have them ready for the week ahead. You can even freeze some of them so you'll be way ahead of the game. Any way you look at it, having these staples on hand to incorporate into your cooking is an easy way to add lots of flavour and flare.

In my family, we like to have our garden herbs dried to enjoy throughout the year. Entering someone's house and discovering a homemade tomato sauce simmering on the stove is a very warm welcome indeed. Getting a step ahead with these staple recipes, used on their own or in other recipes, is part of my Italian heritage that I really cherish. I hope you will, too.

Dried Garden Herbs *Erbe secche dell'orto*

I am not sure what use the furnace has in your house, other than to heat the home of course, but in our family it was always used to help dry laundry, fruit, vegetables and—of course—herbs. We would hang bunches of fresh herbs, plucked from the garden, near the furnace to dry them. For many years, my mother would go to work smelling like oregano as her work clothes hung nearby. It's always nice to wear a natural garden scent to work, you quickly become the favourite!

1 bunch fresh oregano, thyme, rosemary, sage or hearty basil

Look for bush or columnar varieties of herbs to dry. They are a hearty variety that has smaller thicker leaves which are perfect for drying. They retain their flavour and colour well.

LIGHTLY RINSE HERBS and completely pat dry. Remove any brown or spotted leaves.

Divide bunch into sets of 4 or 5 sprigs and tie sprigs together with kitchen string at the cut ends. Hang upside down in a warm room or near a furnace. Let air dry for at least 2 weeks and check to see if herbs are dry and crumbly to the touch. Let dry for more time, if needed.

Remove string and rub dried leaves off stems into paper bag or onto a plate. Rub herbs between your fingers to remove any small stems.

My dad's woodworking hands are perfect for rubbing the leaves off the stems; he can't feel any pain from the rough edges of the dried herbs. If your hands are not as tough as his, be sure to put on some gardening gloves to prevent pricks and picks from the dry stems.

Pack dried herbs in small airtight jars for up to 6 months. Store them in a dark, cool place.

MAKES 1 BUNCH DRIED HERBS.

Depending on the herb used in the recipe, yields may vary. You can get anywhere from 1/4 cup (60 mL) to 1 cup (250 mL) of dried herbs from the original bunch.

Chicken Stock *Brodo di Pollo*

No need to add salt to this stock, all the flavour comes from the chicken and vegetables. Portion it out into convenient containers for you to pull out from the freezer when you need it. Freezable storage containers or ice cube trays work well.

I use the whole chicken when making stock so I have meat to add to soups. The chicken meat is so tender, it's perfect for sandwiches and salads. It's like having two meals cooked in one pot. To make a simple chicken soup, simply add some of the cooked meat from the chicken into the stock with some soup pasta; simmer until the pasta is tender.

1–3 lb (1.5 kg) whole chicken

2 carrots, chopped

2 stalks celery, chopped

1 leek, white and light green parts only,
   halved lengthwise, cut in half and
   washed thoroughly

1 large onion, coarsely chopped

6 cloves garlic

¼ bunch fresh Italian parsley

4 bay leaves

IN A LARGE STOCKPOT, combine all ingredients. Add enough water to cover 2 inches (5 cm) above chicken and vegetables, about 12 cups (3 L); bring to a boil. Skim any foam that forms in the first 15 minutes after the stock begins to boil. Reduce heat and simmer for about 3 hours or until chicken begins to fall apart.

Remove chicken to large plate and let cool. Strain stock and vegetables through a fine meshed sieve into another pot or large bowl. Skim fat from stock or refrigerate overnight and remove fat that forms on the top with a slotted spoon.

Remove meat from bones and reserve for another use. Discard bones.

Divide stock among smaller 2 cup (500 mL) containers (that works best for my freezer) and freeze for up to 6 months. Let thaw in refrigerator, defrost in microwave or warm in saucepan when ready to use.

MAKES ABOUT 12 CUPS (3 L) STOCK AND ABOUT 1 LB (450 G) BOILED CHICKEN MEAT.

Vegetable Stock Option: Omit chicken and use an additional leek.

Place vegetables on parchment paper-lined baking sheet and roast in 400°F (200°C) oven for about 40 minutes or until golden.

Add all ingredients to stockpot and add enough water to cover 1 inch (2.5 cm) above vegetables, about 4 cups (1 L); bring to boil. Reduce heat and simmer for about 1 hour or until vegetables are very soft. Strain and store as above. **MAKES 4 CUPS (1 L).**

Homemade Tomato Sauce *Sugo Fatto in Casa*

This is as close to my mom and Nonna's sauce that I could get. Using homemade canned tomatoes makes a difference but many people don't get a chance to can their own tomatoes. I wanted to be able to offer you a recipe for a tomato sauce using store-bought canned tomatoes that was easy to make and still tasted great.

This sauce is perfect for pasta or any other dish that uses tomato sauce, like pizza (see recipes p. 92, 97 and 98). It's simple and tasty and also freezes beautifully.

2 cans (28 oz / 796 mL) plum tomatoes
6 sprigs fresh Italian parsley
2 sprigs fresh basil
1 small onion, halved
2 cloves garlic, halved
3 Tbsp (45 mL) extra virgin olive oil
1 Tbsp (15 mL) dried oregano leaves
2 tsp (10 mL) salt
¼ tsp (1 mL) hot pepper flakes

You can use 6 cups (1.5 L) of homemade tomatoes if you can your own. You can also use 2 jars (700 mL) of tomato passata if you don't want to puree them yourself.

IN A FOOD MILL OR BLENDER, puree tomatoes until smooth and pour into large saucepan. Add parsley, basil, onion, garlic, oil, oregano, salt and hot pepper flakes. Bring to a boil. Cover and reduce heat to medium-low; cook for about 2 hours or until reduced slightly and thickened.

MAKES 5 CUPS (1.25 L) SAUCE.

You can serve up the very soft onion, garlic and herbs on crusty bread. I have family members that enjoy them this way.

Roasted Tomatoes *Pomodori Arrostiti*

It is a family tradition to buy bushels of tomatoes to make pasta sauce each year. It is an easy way to save money and enjoy the in-season flavour of tomatoes year round. I always take away about half a bushel to make roasted tomatoes to store away in the freezer. Sweet, dark roasted tomatoes retain a slight juiciness to them. On their own, sit them atop a sliced baguette that has been spread with ricotta or goat cheese for an easy appetizer or add them to soups, stews or pasta dishes.

2 lb (1 kg) plum tomatoes, about 20
   (all about the same size)
¼ cup (60 mL) extra virgin olive oil

2 tsp (10 mL) finely chopped fresh basil
2 tsp (10 mL) finely chopped fresh
   oregano

PREHEAT OVEN TO 400°F (200°C).

Line baking sheet with parchment paper; set aside.

Cut tomatoes in half horizontally and trim stem end off. Place cut side up on prepared baking sheet.

In a small bowl, stir together oil, basil and oregano. Brush tomatoes with oil mixture. Roast for about 1 hour and 15 minutes or until very soft and dark golden.
Let cool completely.

MAKES 40 TOMATO HALVES.

Place tomatoes in an airtight container, lining each layer with parchment or waxed paper. Close lid and refrigerate for up to 2 weeks or freeze for up to 3 months.

These are best when in-season, ripe, juicy tomatoes are used.

Balsamic Variation: Reduce oil to 2 Tbsp (30 mL) and add 2 Tbsp (30 mL) balsamic vinegar. These tomatoes will be very dark.

Roasted Red Peppers *Peperoni Rossi Arrostiti*

Each summer the abundance of Ontario's farmed red peppers is wonderful to take advantage of. It's worth picking up a bushel and taking them home to roast or turn into a sauce. Long Sheppard peppers are great as they have fewer seeds in them and a meaty flesh that is full of flavour.

30 sweet red bell or Sheppard peppers
(approx. 11 lb / 5 kg), washed

ALLOW PEPPERS TO DRY. Preheat your grill or barbecue to medium-high heat. Fill the grill with peppers and close lid. Grill for 15 to 25 minutes, turning often, until skins are blistered and charred. Remove to a large bowl or baking sheet and repeat with remaining peppers.

Let cool until peppers are easy enough to handle and remove skins and seeds (don't worry if there are some seeds sticking). Place peppers into small resealable bags, about 3 or 4 per bag and press out the air. Lay flat and freeze for up to 1 year.

When you want to use them, simply let them come to room temperature or let thaw in the refrigerator overnight.

MAKES 10 PACKAGES.

Roasted Red Pepper Sauce: Puree roasted red peppers in a blender or food processor until smooth and freeze in airtight containers or resealable bags for up to 1 year.

Red Pepper Sauce *Salsa di Peperoni Rossi Arrostiti*

This variation allows you to make a fresh tasting red pepper sauce without roasting them. You can use this method for hot peppers as well.

8 sweet red bell or Sheppard peppers
  (approx. 3 lb / 1.5 kg)

CUT PEPPERS IN HALF and remove seeds. Cut into large pieces. Place in a large pot and fill bottom with water to steam peppers.

Bring to a boil, cover and steam for about 25 minutes or until very soft. Drain well and place in food processor. Puree until smooth. Divide into airtight containers or resealable bags and freeze for up to 6 months.

MAKES 4 CUPS (1 L).

For longer storage, place the sauce in canning jars and process them in a hot water bath.

Fresh Creamy Ricotta Cheese

Ricotta Fresca e Cremosa

This rich tasting ricotta is perfect to enjoy fresh and this amount is just right to enjoy with a group of people. All it needs is a little sprinkle of fresh ground pepper and crostini or crackers to serve alongside or serve warm with a drizzle of chestnut or buckwheat honey, a favourite of mine.

4 cups (1 L) 1% milk
1 cup (250 mL) 35% whipping cream
½ tsp (2 mL) salt
¼ cup (60 mL) lemon juice

For best results, do not use microfiltered milk for the recipe.

IN A SAUCEPAN, bring milk, cream and salt to a gentle boil over medium-high heat, stirring occasionally. Stir in lemon juice, reduce heat and simmer, stirring for about 5 minutes or until small curds are visible. Let stand for 5 minutes. Pour into a cheese cloth-lined sieve, reserving whey for another use if desired. Let ricotta stand for 10 minutes or drain.

MAKES 1 CUP (250 ML).

If you would like double the amount of ricotta, simply make another batch separately to retain the rich and creamy consistency.

EASTER

For Italians, this holiday is just as important as Christmas when it comes to food. The get-togethers are fabulous and the food served speaks for itself. I love all of the traditions that I was raised with. For instance, having no meat on Good Friday is a long standing tradition in our home. Another tradition is that all of the aunts get together to help with the baking, ensuring that there is enough to be shared with other family members at dinner or after Mass.

I remember Easter weekend being filled with many visits to church. Nonno was a Lay Minister of the Roman Catholic Church so it was cool to see him up at the front of the altar, handing out communion.

Did I enjoy getting dressed up for church? Not a chance! As a little girl who didn't enjoy putting on party dresses, the pastel coloured Easter dresses with matching hats that my mother bought were not my cup of tea. They were beautiful, as everyone pointed out, but I never really liked the attention that came with them. Having my younger sister in a matching outfit didn't sit well with me either.

The large chocolate Easter eggs were always the biggest hit of the weekend. Every great aunt and uncle would show up with one for the kids. We loved the little plastic trinkets that were found inside the eggs and I remember the slightly waxy taste of those eggs like it was yesterday. We were happy to indulge in chocolate all weekend long!

Sometimes the meals were simple, a pasta or soup to start and then roast lamb with potatoes and a salad. Other times the dinners went on for hours as we enjoyed many courses. No one ever minded because it gave us plenty of time to catch up and enjoy each other's company. The women would collect the dirty dishes and head off to the kitchen. Men would sit and enjoy each other's company while the kids ran around, no doubt full of energy from all of the chocolate eggs!

It was usually an early bedtime on Easter Sunday after all of the excitement of having family over and enjoying the delicious food throughout the weekend.

These spring-inspired meals are wonderful to make any time during the season but they are particularly special around Easter. Check out the menu suggestions on page 16 or create your own menu for your family get-together.

Egg and Raisin Bread *Pane all'Uvetta e all'Uovo*

Easter is when we eat the most delicious breads; braided, shaped and twisted into beautiful gifts to share with family. I remember standing beside my Nonna to get every measure for this recipe. I drove her nuts that day, but it was worth it to be able to share this delicious recipe.

You can double this recipe and have some for the freezer. This bread freezes beautifully and is a great gift for family and friends. I enjoy serving this bread with coffee or simply toasted with butter. It also makes a great French toast for brunch!

1 cup (250 mL) sugar, divided
½ cup (125 mL) warm water
1 Tbsp (15 mL) active dry yeast
1 cup (250 mL) + 1 Tbsp (15 mL) milk
3 eggs
½ cup (125 mL) butter, melted
1 Tbsp (15 mL) orange zest
¼ tsp (1 mL) anise extract (optional)
5 cups (1.25 L) all-purpose flour (approx.)
1 tsp (5 mL) salt
½ cup (125 mL) golden raisins, soaked

To soak the raisins, simply pour boiling water over raisins to cover and let stand for 10 minutes until ready to use. Drain before using.

Egg Wash
1 egg
1 Tbsp (15 mL) milk

IN A BOWL, DISSOLVE 2 TSP (10 mL) of the sugar into warm water. Sprinkle with yeast and let stand for 10 minutes or until frothy. Whisk in milk.

In another bowl, whisk together 3 eggs and remaining sugar, butter, orange zest and anise extract, if using. Whisk into milk mixture.

CONTINUED NEXT PAGE >

Egg and Raisin Bread CONTINUED

In a large bowl, stir together flour and salt. Pour yeast mixture over flour mixture stirring to make a soft slightly sticky dough. Stir in raisins. Scrape dough onto floured work surface and knead to make soft smooth dough, adding more flour if dough is sticky. Place dough in oiled bowl. Cover and let rise in warm place for about 1 hour or until doubled in size. Punch down dough and divide into 4 or 6 balls. Roll out each ball of dough as desired and place on parchment paper-lined baking sheets or in greased baking pans and let rise for about 1 hour or until doubled in volume.

Preheat oven to 350°F (180°C).

Brush loaves with egg wash and bake in oven for about 30 minutes or until golden brown. Let cool slightly before removing from pan to cool completely.

Egg Wash: To make egg wash, mix egg with milk and beat well.

MAKES 4 TO 6 LOAVES.

Ricotta Ball Soup *Zuppa con Polpette di Ricotta*

Dumplings can be made with many different ingredients and each culture has one. This southern Italian favourite always hit the spot during cold winter months while we were waiting for spring to arrive. As Easter bounces around the calendar, this soup can be made anytime. Traditionally a starter soup to the Easter meal, it is light and flavourful. The ricotta balls are moist and delicate which makes spooning the soup into your mouth that much more enjoyable.

8 cups (2 L) chicken or vegetable stock
   (see recipe p. 22)
⅓ cup (80 mL) chopped fresh Italian parsley
1 tub (475 g) ricotta
1 cup (250 mL) dry bread crumbs (approx.)
1 egg
⅓ cup (80 mL) grated mozzarella cheese
¼ cup (60 mL) fresh grated Parmesan cheese
¼ tsp (1 mL) salt

You will need 1½ cups (375 mL) of ricotta cheese for this recipe.

Look for dry bread crumbs in the bakery aisle of your local grocery store.

IN A LARGE SOUP POT or Dutch oven, bring chicken or vegetable stock and 3 Tbsp (50 mL) of the parsley to boil; reduce heat to a simmer.

Meanwhile, in a large bowl, stir together ricotta, bread crumbs, mozzarella cheese, remaining parsley, Parmesan cheese and salt until mixture sticks together. Add more bread crumbs if necessary to keep mixture together.

Using a ¼ cup (60 mL) dry measure, scoop out ricotta mixture and gently shape into balls. Using a slotted spoon, place ricotta balls into chicken stock. Return stock to a gentle boil; cook for about 10 minutes or until ricotta balls are firm throughout.

MAKES 4 TO 6 SERVINGS.

Balsamic Lamb Chops *Costolette di Agnello al Balsamico*

This is my fallback for an appetizer or main course when family and friends come over. It has appeared at so many family functions and holidays that many have asked me for the recipe. I had never really written it down and just made it in the moment, which is how most Italian recipes begin. This recipe is inspired by delicious lamb chops I had at a cousin's home in Calabria. They are super easy to make.

4 racks of lamb, trimmed and cut into
   chops (about 3–4 lb / 1.5–2 kg total)
3 Tbsp (45 mL) extra virgin olive oil
2 Tbsp (30 mL) Dijon mustard
1 Tbsp (15 mL) chopped fresh rosemary

2 tsp (10 mL) chopped fresh thyme
3 cloves garlic, minced
½ tsp (2 mL) salt
½ tsp (2 mL) fresh ground pepper
1 batch Balsamic Glaze (see recipe p. 93)

PLACE LAMB CHOPS IN A LARGE BOWL. Add oil, mustard, rosemary, thyme, garlic, salt and pepper and using your hands, toss together to coat the lamb chops well. Cover and refrigerate for at least 30 minutes or up to 24 hours.

Preheat grill to medium-high and oil or spray lightly. Place chops on grill, turning once, for about 8 minutes or until medium rare. Cook them longer if you wish, but I enjoy them with some pink inside. Remove to a large platter and drizzle with balsamic glaze to serve.

MAKES 36 PIECES OR 4 TO 6 SERVINGS.

Ricotta Cheesecake with Caramel Sauce

Torta di Ricotta con Caramello

Celebrating Easter is a big deal for many Italians. The enjoyment of meeting up for a celebratory lunch after Palm Sunday is something I always remember. This dessert uses ricotta cheese which is widely used in dishes that are both sweet and savoury in Southern Italian meals. This ricotta cheesecake has a different texture than regular cheesecake and offers up a wonderful flavour. This cake is big enough to feed a crowd.

2 tubs (475 g each) ricotta cheese
1 cup (250 mL) Mascarpone cheese
1 cup (250 mL) icing sugar
⅓ cup (80 mL) sugar
2 tsp (10 mL) grated orange zest
⅓ cup (80 mL) orange juice
4 eggs

You will need 3 cups (750 mL) of ricotta for the recipe.

Caramel Sauce
⅔ cup (160 mL) packed brown sugar
⅓ cup (80 mL) butter
⅓ cup (80 mL) whipping cream

PREHEAT OVEN TO 375°F (190°C). Wrap just the outside of a 9-inch (23 cm) springform pan with foil.

In a large bowl using an electric mixer, beat ricotta and Mascarpone cheeses with sugars until combined and smooth. Beat in orange zest and juice. Beat in eggs, one at a time, beating well after each addition.

Pour cheese mixture into pan and bake in oven for about 1 hour or until top is golden and centre is still slightly jiggly. Turn oven off and let stand in oven for 30 minutes. Remove from oven and let cool to room temperature. Refrigerate for at least 4 hours before serving.

Caramel Sauce: In a small saucepan, combine sugar, butter and cream over medium heat. Bring to a boil and boil gently, whisking for about 1 minute or until smooth. Let cool to room temperature. Serve with cheesecake.

MAKES 12 TO 16 SERVINGS.

This can be made and stored in the refrigerator for up to 2 days. Warm sauce before serving over low heat, stirring occasionally.

Candied Orange Ricotta Tart
Crostata di Ricotta con Arancia Caramellata

This rich cheesecake is known as a *crostata*, like most cake or tart-like desserts in Italy. I like to add the orange flavour of candied fruit and zest but it is equally delicious with lemon or lime zest.

1½ cups (375 mL) all-purpose flour
¼ cup (60 mL) sugar
2 tsp (10 mL) lemon zest
Pinch of salt
½ cup (125 mL) butter, cubed
1 egg, lightly beaten
1 Tbsp (15 mL) water (optional)

Filling
1 tub (475 g) ricotta cheese
½ cup (125 mL) whipping cream
2 eggs
⅓ cup (80 mL) sugar
¼ cup (60 mL) finely chopped candied orange peel
1 Tbsp (15 mL) orange zest
1 tsp (5 mL) lemon zest
1 tsp (5 mL) vanilla
⅓ cup (80 mL) slivered almonds

IN A LARGE BOWL, combine flour, sugar, lemon zest and salt. Add butter and, using your hands, combine with flour until coarse crumbs form. Add egg and mix with hands until dough starts to hold together. Add water, if necessary. Scrape onto floured surface and knead gently to form smooth dough. Reserve one-quarter of the dough and wrap with plastic wrap; refrigerate.

Preheat oven to 375°F (190°C).

Roll remaining dough out to fit into 9-inch (23 cm) tart pan with removable bottom. Refrigerate for about 30 minutes or until firm. Prick bottom of tart with fork and line with foil. Fill with pie weights or dried beans and bake in bottom third of oven for about 25 minutes or until light golden. Let cool.

Filling: While tart shell is baking, in large bowl and using electric mixer, beat ricotta cheese, whipping cream, eggs and sugar until well combined. Stir in candied orange, fruit zests and vanilla. Scrape filling into baked tart shell and spread evenly. Sprinkle with almonds.

Roll out reserved dough on floured surface and cut into ½-inch (1 cm) strips. Overlap strips in a lattice pattern over top of ricotta mixture. Bake in oven for about 45 minutes or until puffed and filling is slightly jiggly in centre. Let cool completely before serving.

MAKES 8 SERVINGS.

Cream-Filled Doughnuts *Zeppole*

When I lived in Vaughan, just north of Toronto, celebrating St Joseph on March 19 was one of my favourite days of the year because all the Italian bakeries were full of *zeppole*. It usually falls before or very close to Easter. St. Joseph is celebrated and those that have Joseph in their name, or a derivative of it, also celebrate.

Typically in the late winter you will see bakery windows filled with these delicious cream-filled pastries. They are perfect to enjoy with an espresso and to share with family. You can fry or bake the pastry and although I am a big fan of frying dough, this baked version is delicious and looks spectacular.

1 cup (250 mL) water
⅓ cup (80 mL) butter
1 cup (250 mL) all-purpose flour
2 tsp (10 mL) sugar
4 eggs

1 batch Lemon Cream, chilled (see recipe p. 197)
3–6 Black cherries (fresh, frozen or canned), quartered or halved if smaller
2 tsp (10 mL) Icing sugar

PREHEAT OVEN TO 425°F (220°C). Line 2 baking sheets with parchment paper; set aside.

Bring water and butter to boil in a saucepan. Stir together flour and sugar in a bowl. Add to water mixture and stir all at once with a wooden spoon to combine and form a ball in the saucepan. Cook, stirring over medium heat, for about 1 minute or until mixture has a smooth mashed potato-like consistency. Remove from heat and scrape into a large bowl. Let cool slightly.

Beat in eggs, one at a time, using an electric mixer until a stretchy, sticky dough forms. Scrape dough into a piping bag fitted with a star attachment or use a spoon. Make 12 round wreaths, about 2 inches (5 cm) apart, on prepared baking sheets. Using a wet finger, smooth tops.

Bake in top and bottom third of oven for 20 minutes, alternating pans halfway through. Reduce heat to 350°F (180°C) and, using a small paring knife, poke small hole on the side of each puff. Bake for about 5 minutes or until light golden. Let cool completely and slice in half.

Fill each wreath with cream and return top to each. Dollop small amounts of custard around the top and decorate with cherries. Refrigerate for up to 1 day and sprinkle with icing sugar before serving.

MAKES 12 SERVINGS

Hard Genettis *Genetti*

It is difficult to discover what this sweet's true identity is. In our house we call them genetti, even though there is another cookie with the same name, which is completely different in texture and shape. For some, this cookie is known as *Taralli all'Uovo*, which means "oval made with eggs." It is part of old Italian culture to make these for Easter. This is why I love the Italian culture so much—recipes are different based on where and who they come from and sometimes what day it is!

6 eggs
1½ tsp (7 mL) canola oil
½ tsp (2 mL) baking powder
Pinch of salt
2¾ cups (675 mL) all-purpose flour,
   divided

Glaze
3 cups (750 mL) icing sugar
¼ cup (60 mL) milk (approx.)

IN A LARGE BOWL, whisk together eggs, oil, baking powder and salt. Stir in 2½ cups (625 mL) flour until firm dough starts to form. Place dough on floured surface and knead in the remaining ¼ cup (60 mL) of flour until pliable soft but smooth firm dough forms.

Divide dough into 6 equal pieces and roll into a 12-inch (30 cm) rope. Pinch ends together to form a small circle.

Bring a large pot of water to boil and gently add the dough circles a couple at a time, turning and boiling for about 2 minutes or until they float to the top. Remove to a clean tea towel and repeat with remaining circles.

Preheat oven to 350°F (180°C).

Using a small knife, cut a small slit around the centre but not all the way through, in the side of the circle on the outside.

Bake circles directly on the middle rack for about 20 minutes or until light golden and crisp. Remove to rack to cool completely. Cut each genetti into 4–6 pieces.

> Be sure to move them around in the oven to bake evenly in case there are hot spots in your oven.

Glaze: In a bowl, whisk together icing sugar and milk (adding more if necessary for a slightly thickened but runny glaze) and brush each genetti with glaze to coat and set aside to harden.

MAKES 24 PIECES.

Ricotta Cannoli *Cannoli di Ricotta*

There are so many variations for cannoli filling that you can create different varieties as you are making them. You can buy the cannoli shells in most grocery stores but you will always find them in an Italian deli or grocer. I love making a bunch and then sneaking one out of the fridge to enjoy with an espresso before guests arrive; they are a perfect little pick me up served together. These are so easy you will be making them every weekend for guests and family. You can vary your filling by using candied mixed fruit, chopped glazed cherries or lemon zest.

1 tub (475 g) smooth ricotta cheese
½ cup (125 mL) + 2 tsp (10 mL) icing sugar
½ cup (125 mL) miniature chocolate chips
½ tsp (2 mL) vanilla extract
18–24 cannoli shells
18–24 maraschino cherry halves (optional)

You will need 1½ cups (375 mL) of ricotta for this recipe.

Look for cannoli shells packed in a single layer for less breakage. Most bakeries carry cannoli shells, if they are not on store shelves simply ask at the counter and they may be able to order them for you.

IN A LARGE BOWL, stir together ricotta cheese and ½ cup (125 mL) icing sugar until combined. Stir in chocolate chips and vanilla. Pipe or spoon ricotta mixture into shells. Place 1 maraschino cherry half on each end of cannoli, if using. Cover and refrigerate for at least 1 hour or overnight. (The longer they are refrigerated the softer the cannoli shells will get.)

Sprinkle with remaining icing sugar before serving.

MAKES 18 TO 24 CANNOLI.

Cheese-Filled Sicilian Cake *Cassata Siciliana*

This Sicilian dessert is a sponge cake filled with a ricotta filling similar to cannoli. Traditionally this dessert was made around Easter by nuns and has become a favourite throughout Southern Italy in home kitchens. Many also recognize *cassata* as an ice cream flavour that is filled with candied fruit peels, nuts and sometimes chocolate. It is made like an ice cream cake, so substitute your favourite Italian "gelato" ice cream, like spumoni, for the filling.

1 tub (475 g) extra smooth ricotta cheese

10 oz (300 g) frozen pound cake, thawed

⅓ cup (80 mL) cherry brandy, divided

½ cup (125 mL) sugar

¾ cup (190 mL) mini chocolate chips

½ cup (125 mL) chopped candied
   mixed fruit

⅓ cup (80 mL) shelled pistachios, chopped

¼ tsp (1 mL) ground cinnamon (optional)

3.5 oz (100 g) marzipan

1 cup (250 mL) whipping cream

2 Tbsp (30 mL) icing sugar

Candied fruit for garnish (as much as you like)

You will need 1½ cups (375 mL) of ricotta for this recipe.

Marzipan is often sold in 200 g packages, so half of one is perfect for this recipe.

PLACE RICOTTA IN A FINE MESH SIEVE and drain over bowl; set aside. Line 8-inch (20 cm) round cake pan with plastic wrap leaving overhang around edge of pan.

Cut cake into thin ¼-inch (6 mm) slices and line bottom and sides of pan, trimming cake as necessary. Brush cake with about half of the brandy; set aside.

In a bowl, whisk drained ricotta cheese and sugar together until creamy. Stir in chocolate chips, candied fruit, pistachios, cinnamon and 1 Tbsp (15 mL) of the brandy, if using, until well combined. Scrape into cake-lined pan and smooth top.

Using a rolling pin dusted with icing sugar roll out marzipan into a circle to fit into pan. Place on top of ricotta mixture. Brush some of the brandy over marzipan and top with remaining cake slices, trimming to fit. Brush remaining brandy on cake slices. Press down gently and cover with plastic wrap. Refrigerate for at least 2 hours or up to 24 hours.

Before serving, whip cream with icing sugar. Turn cake out onto cake plate and spread whipped cream over cake to cover. Smooth out decoratively and pipe with any remaining whipped cream. Garnish with candied fruit.

MAKES 12 SERVINGS.

Muzzi Family Genetti *Genetti della Famiglia Muzzi*

These traditional Easter cookies are made in many southern Italian households. These genetti are lighter in texture than other versions in this book. Natalina Muzzi, the matriarch of my cousin Aldo's family, made these delicate and light cookies that people would travel from all over just to get a taste of. She would also carefully package them up for her children to take with them to share with her grandchildren when they couldn't make the trip. Now, these are not as perfect as hers (how could they be?), but I love their light airy texture and I'm happy to share the story of her great Italian legacy. I hope everyone gets to have one.

6 eggs
½ cup (125 mL) sugar
Pinch of salt
2 tsp (10 mL) brandy

½ cup (125 mL) canola oil
2½ cups (625 mL) all-purpose flour
2 Tbsp (30 mL) baking powder

PREHEAT OVEN TO 350°F (180°C). Line 2 baking sheets with parchment paper; set aside.

In a large bowl, beat together eggs, sugar and salt until sugar dissolves and the mixture takes on a light colour.

Beat in brandy and oil until well blended. Stir in flour and baking powder until soft dough forms. This dough should not be stiff.

Using a tablespoon or mini ice cream scoop, scoop out dough onto prepared baking sheets about 2 inches (5 cm) apart.

Bake in oven for about 7 minutes or until very light golden and just firm.

MAKES 4 DOZEN COOKIES.

If you want to glaze these cookies, you can drizzle a little bit of milk or water into some icing sugar and brush over the cookies. For added flavour, add a drop of vanilla or anisette to the glaze.

You can also check out the Genetti recipe on page 49 for an easy icing.

Genetti Cookies *Genetti*

I love these cookies because they represent an Easter family tradition. There is no explanation as to why we make these cookies, I just know that ever since I can remember, we have made them for Easter. Anytime I make them, the thought of spring and Easter is strong. They are easy to make and great to dunk into coffee. This is my Nonna's recipe with a hint of additional flavouring. My kids adore them and I make these genetti for them now, too. You can change the flavour of these cookies to suit your needs. My favourite is easy and simple but lemon or orange zest works perfectly, too.

3 eggs
½ cup (125 mL) vegetable oil
½ cup (125 mL) sugar
½ tsp (2 mL) anise liqueur or anisette
   flavouring or vanilla
2 cups (500 mL) all-purpose flour (approx.)
2 Tbsp (30 mL) baking powder
Pinch of salt

Icing
1 cup (250 mL) icing sugar
2 Tbsp (30 mL) butter, softened
2 Tbsp (30 mL) milk
½ tsp (2 mL) vanilla

IN A LARGE BOWL, whisk together eggs and oil until combined. Beat in sugar until frothy and dissolved into eggs. Whisk in flavouring.

In another bowl, whisk together flour, baking powder and salt. Add to egg mixture and stir to make soft dough.

Preheat oven to 375°F (190°C). Line baking sheets with parchment paper; set aside.

Roll pieces of dough into about 6-inch (15 cm) long, pencil thin ropes and cross over to form a twisted shape. Place on parchment paper-lined baking sheets and repeat with remaining dough.

Bake for about 10 minutes or until light golden on the bottom. Let cool.

Icing: In a bowl, whisk together icing sugar, butter, milk and vanilla until smooth. Spread or dip each cookie into icing and let stand for about 1 hour or until set.

MAKES 4 DOZEN COOKIES.

CHRISTMAS

During the Christmas season, there are many traditions that Southern Italians have, which differ from family to family. In our house, we celebrate *La Vigilia* (Christmas Eve) with my parents and we enjoy a family fish dinner. The Feast of Seven Fishes, known as *La Festa Dei Sette Pesci* in Italian, happens on Christmas Eve. Traditionally seven fish dishes are served to celebrate the seven Catholic sacraments.

In my family we are happy with three or four fish courses. We usually start with vegetable and cheese antipasti, then a soup and a pasta dish that include seafood. Follow that up with three or four fish dishes, each prepared differently, finished by a crisp green salad and a little dessert later on.

There are many stories as to why fish is served instead of meat on Christmas Eve, the most practical reason being that not eating meat on the night before Holy days is part of the Roman Catholic tradition.

Getting all of this food ready requires many hands and lots of kitchen space. My parents have always had a second kitchen in the basement for this exact situation. My mother sneaks downstairs to fry up the fish so the rest of us don't have to endure the smell. It's never bothered me as I love what comes from all of the effort and my kids are the same way. The mom's recipe for Fritto Misto (see recipe p. 62) is always a big hit with her grand-kids.

At Christmastime, there is never a lack of good food. Whether it's roasting chestnuts, baking cookies or frying up treats like Scallili (page 66), it all brings a smile to my face. There are always mandarins on the table, as well as torrone (nougat), panettone (Italian Christmas sweet bread), stuffed figs and gianduia (a soft hazelnut-flavoured chocolate). Truly a feast for the senses.

At this time of year, everyone is busy so we all pitch in to get things done; setting the table, stirring pots and washing dishes, just to name a few. Everyone contributes so that we can all be together, enjoying delicious meals during the festive season.

I believe that food is one of the best ways for kids to understand their culture. Foods like Cudduri (see recipe p. 53) represent our family's heritage and our love of food and family. These holiday traditions will be valued and hopefully carried on for generations to come through our children and our children's children.

Potato Doughnuts *Cudduri / Grispelle / Cullurielli*

There are so many names for this Italian variation of the doughnut that I am not sure what to call it other than a doughnut! During the holiday season when family gets together it is wonderful to set aside a day to make these tasty treats. If you want to save some for a later date, my recommendation is to freeze them once they are cool so they don't get too chewy and tough. Some members of my family (who will not be named) enjoy the chewiness and are sad when they are fluffy; they are in the minority. I have always enjoyed these. My dad and some family members enjoy tucking a little sardines or anchovies into the dough before it's fried to give it a savoury salty fish flavour. My kids and husband enjoy a heavy sprinkle of cinnamon and sugar for a sweet treat. The classic way my Nonna made them was dipped in honey. Christmas isn't the same without them.

4 potatoes (about 1¼ lb / 600 g total weight), peeled and chopped

2 Tbsp (30 mL) salt

2½ cups (625 mL) warm water, divided

2 Tbsp (30 mL) active dry yeast

6 cups (1.5 mL) + 2 tsp (10 mL) canola oil

9 cups (2.25 L) all-purpose flour (approx.), divided

1 cup (250 mL) honey (optional)

¾ cup (180 mL) sugar (optional)

1 Tbsp (15 mL) cinnamon (optional)

IN A POT OF BOILING WATER, cook potatoes for about 20 minutes or until very tender. Drain well; add salt and mash until fairly smooth. Set aside.

In a very large bowl, combine ½ cup (125 mL) water with yeast and let stand for 10 minutes or until frothy. Stir in remaining water, 2 tsp (10 mL) oil and mashed potatoes. Stir in 5 cups (1.25 L) flour to form a ragged dough. Dump dough out onto floured surface and continue kneading in flour until a smooth, not sticky, dough forms.

Place in large oiled bowl or leave on counter, covered, with a clean tea towel for 2 hours or until doubled in size. Divide dough into 4 pieces.

Working with 1 piece at a time, divide into 8–12 pieces. Roll each piece out into a long smooth rope and join to form a circle. Place on lightly floured tea towel or tablecloth and repeat with remaining dough. Let stand for 30 minutes.

Meanwhile, heat oil in a large deep heavy saucepan to 350–365°F (180–185°C). Carefully place doughnuts into oil, a few at a time, turning occasionally for 4 minutes or until golden brown and cooked through. Remove to paper towel-lined baking sheet and repeat with remaining doughnuts. Heat honey to dip doughnuts in or roll them while still warm in a mixture of cinnamon and sugar. These are best eaten the day they are made.

MAKES 3 TO 4 DOZEN DOUGHNUTS.

Seafood Salad *Insalate di Frutta di Mare*

My husband and I love going out for dinner. Italian eateries are always our favourite and we try to order things we haven't tried. For a long time, we would visit Grazie Ristorante, an Italian restaurant in Toronto and he would order the seafood salad. I loved it and thought this would be a great one to recreate at home and use for holiday fare at our Christmas Eve fish dinner. This is a cold salad that is perfect for antipasto or to serve on a larger scale for people to help themselves. This needs to be made ahead to enjoy the full flavour of the seafood and citrus flavours.

3 calamari (squid) tubes, cleaned (about
   10 oz / 300 g)
6 large scallops
4 oz (125 g) medium raw shrimp, peeled
   and deveined
¼ cup (60 mL) extra virgin olive oil
4 cloves garlic, minced
¼ tsp (1 mL) hot pepper flakes
1 jar (750 mL) pickled mixed vegetables,
   drained and chopped coarsely

¼ cup (60 mL) slivered green olives
¼ cup (60 mL) chopped Italian parsley
1 Tbsp (15 mL) capers
2 Tbsp (25 mL) white vinegar
2 Tbsp (25 mL) lemon juice
Pinch of salt
Pinch of pepper
6–8 leaf lettuce leaves

SLICE CALAMARI BODY into 1-inch (2.5 cm) wide rings and separate tentacles. Cut scallops into quarters and shrimp in half.

In a saucepan full of simmering water, cook calamari for 1 minute. Remove with slotted spoon. Repeat with shrimp and scallops; set aside.

In a skillet, heat oil over medium heat and cook garlic for 30 seconds. Add calamari, shrimp, scallops and hot pepper flakes. Toss and cook for 2 minutes. Scrape into large bowl. Add pickled vegetables, olives, parsley and capers and toss to combine. Add vinegar, lemon juice, salt and pepper and toss well. Cover and refrigerate for at least 1 hour or for up to 12 hours. Serve on lettuce.

MAKES 6 TO 8 SERVINGS.

Seafood Stuffed Shells

Conchiglie Ripiene con Frutta di Mare

I love stuffed pasta. With seafood it becomes an exquisite dish that can be brought to Nonna's house for a traditional Christmas Eve fish dinner or it can be served up for a celebratory New Year's Eve party. These shells are a luxurious way to enjoy crab and shrimp. Try it also with lobster or chopped scallops, if desired.

Creamy Herb Sauce

¼ cup (60 mL) butter

⅓ cup (80 mL) all-purpose flour

4 cups (1 L) milk

8 oz (225 g) package cream cheese, cubed ⎯⎯

¼ cup (60 mL) chopped fresh basil

2 Tbsp (30 mL) chopped fresh Italian
  parsley

2 Tbsp (30 mL) chopped fresh chives

2 tsp (10 mL) lemon zest

½ tsp (2 mL) salt

½ tsp (2 mL) black pepper

One package of cream cheese is equivalent to 1 cup (250 mL)

Shells

24–30 jumbo pasta shells

1 lb (450 g) small cooked shrimp, finely
  chopped

1 lb (450 g) cooked crabmeat

3 cups (750 mL) cooked broccoli, chopped

½ cup (125 mL) fresh grated Parmesan
  cheese

Creamy Herb Sauce: In a saucepan, melt butter over medium heat. Whisk in flour and cook for 1 minute. Gradually whisk in milk and bring to a boil. Reduce heat to medium-low and cook for 10 minutes or until thickened to coat back of spoon. Remove from heat and stir in cream cheese, basil, parsley, chives, lemon zest, salt and pepper until smooth. Set aside.

To make a Creamy Rose Herb Sauce, stir in 1/2 cup (125 mL) of a tomato-based pasta sauce into the cream sauce before using.

Shells: In a large pot of boiling salted water, cook shells for about 7 minutes or until *al dente*. Drain and rinse under cold water. Place in a single layer on damp tea towel. Preheat oven to 400°F (200°C). Grease a 13 × 9-inch (33 × 23 cm) casserole dish; set aside.

Set aside 2 cups (500 mL) of the creamy herb sauce and add broccoli and seafood to remaining sauce. Fill shells with broccoli and seafood mixture. Place in prepared casserole dish. Drizzle reserved sauce over top shells and sprinkle with Parmesan. Cover and bake for about 20 minutes. Uncover and bake for 15 minutes longer or until golden and bubbly.

MAKES 8 TO 10 SERVINGS.

Mussel Soup *Zuppa di Cozze*

Mussel soup is great to serve during the busy Italian holiday season. Whether you want to serve it up for Christmas Eve or when guests come for another dinner during the holidays, this simple dish is both rustic and elegant.

2 Tbsp (30 mL) extra virgin olive oil
1 onion, finely chopped
3 cloves garlic, minced
½ tsp (2 mL) hot pepper flakes
½ cup (125 mL) chopped fresh Italian
   parsley, divided
5 lb (2.5 kg) mussels, rinsed
1 cup (250 mL) dry white wine
1 cup (250 mL) chicken or fish stock
2 Tbsp (30 mL) butter, softened
2 Tbsp (30 mL) all-purpose flour
Salt, to taste
1 baguette, sliced and toasted
1 lemon, cut in wedges

Check the mussels before cooking and make sure they are closed tight. You can tap them or pinch them closed to see if they close; if they don't, discard them. Discard any that have cracked or broken shells.

IN A DUTCH OVEN OR LARGE SOUP POT, heat oil over medium heat. Add onion, garlic, hot pepper flakes and half of the parsley; cook for about 3 minutes or until softened. Add wine and stock; bring to a simmer for 10 minutes.

Add mussels, cover and simmer for about 10 minutes or until mussels open. Discard any mussels that do not open.

Divide mussels among large deep bowls; keep warm.

In a small bowl, mix together butter and flour to make a paste. Whisk into mussel liquid and bring to boil. Season with salt, if desired.

Meanwhile, garnish soup with baguette slices and lemon wedges. Pour liquid over mussels and sprinkle with remaining parsley.

MAKES 4 TO 6 SERVINGS.

Cod with Tomatoes and Potatoes
Baccala con Pomodoro e Patate

This is a staple during the holidays or on Fridays when traditionally a lot of fish is eaten. I remember my Nonno loving cod and my Nonna would make some sort of cod dish every Friday. This favourite was served up on Christmas Eve, as part of our traditional fish meal, but was also easy enough to prepare as a weeknight meal.

2 yellow-fleshed potatoes, thinly sliced

2 Tbsp (30 mL) extra virgin olive oil

1 leek, white and light green part only,
   thinly sliced

2 green onions, chopped

2 cloves garlic, minced

1 can (28 oz / 800 mL) plum tomatoes

1 bay leaf

½ tsp (2 mL) salt

½ tsp (2 mL) pepper

1 lb (450 g) fresh cod fillets

You will need about 3 cups (750 mL) of canned plum tomatoes for this recipe.

IN A SMALL SAUCEPAN, cover potatoes with water and bring to a boil. Cook for 10 minutes, drain and set aside.

Meanwhile, in a large saucepan, heat oil over medium heat and cook leek, onions and garlic for about 8 minutes or until softened. Add tomatoes, bay leaf, salt and pepper and bring to boil. Add potatoes and cover and simmer for 15 minutes or until thickened.

Add cod into tomato mixture and stir gently. Cook, uncovered, for about 8 minutes or until cod flakes when tested with fork.

MAKES 4 SERVINGS.

Squash and Hazelnut Rotelle

Rotelle di Zucca e Nocciola

Christmas Eve—or *La Vigilia* as it's known throughout Italian homes—is celebrated with a delicious meal that typically does not include meat. The courses are still filled with texture and flavour even without meat. We start out with pasta after antipasto and this stuffed version is perfect to serve. Swirls of pasta surround the pale orange filling that has added crunch from the hazelnuts.

   This dish can be made in advance. Let cool for 30 minutes and cover before refrigerating for up to 2 days.

**6 cups (1.5 L) butternut squash, peeled
   and cubed**
1 cup (250 mL) ricotta cheese
½ cup (125 mL) toasted hazelnuts, chopped
⅓ cup (80 mL) chopped fresh Italian parsley
¼ cup (60 mL) fresh grated Parmesan cheese
1 small clove garlic, minced
½ tsp (2 mL) fresh ground pepper
¼ tsp (1 mL) salt
4 sheets fresh pasta (see recipe p. 110)

You will need two-thirds of a 475 g tub of ricotta for this recipe.

Rose Sauce

3 Tbsp (45 mL) butter
3 Tbsp (45 mL) all-purpose flour
3 cups (750 mL) milk
**½ cup (125 mL) Homemade tomato sauce
   (see recipe p. 23) or pasta sauce**
½ tsp (2 mL) salt
½ tsp (2 mL) black pepper
Pinch of fresh grated nutmeg
2 Tbsp (30 mL) fresh grated Parmesan cheese

Rolls of pasta can be made a day in advance and wrapped in plastic if you store them in the refrigerator.

IN A LARGE SAUCEPAN OF BOILING WATER, cook squash for about 20 minutes or until tender. Drain and place in a large bowl. Mash squash until smooth. Add ricotta, hazelnuts, parsley, Parmesan cheese, garlic, pepper and salt and stir until combined.

Meanwhile, in a pot of boiling salted water, cook pasta for 2 minutes. Drain and rinse under cold water. Lay a single layer of pasta on a clean tea towel and pat dry. Spread squash mixture evenly over pasta sheets, leaving ½ inch (1 cm) of space on 1 short end. Starting on opposite end, roll up jelly-roll style. Slice each roll into 6 pieces; set aside.

Rose Sauce: In a saucepan, melt butter over medium heat. Add flour and cook, stirring for 1 minute. Whisk in milk and cook, whisking for about 15 minutes or until thick enough to coat back of spoon. Whisk in tomato sauce, salt, pepper and nutmeg.

Preheat oven to 375°F (190°C). Grease a 13 × 9-inch (33 × 23 cm) baking dish.

Pour half of the sauce into baking dish to cover bottom. Place pasta pieces in pan, overlapping slightly. Pour remaining sauce to cover. Sprinkle with cheese. Bake for about 25 minutes or until golden and bubbly.

Make ahead: Let cool 30 minutes. Cover and refrigerate for up to 2 days.

MAKES 8 TO 12 SERVINGS.

Fried Mixed Fish *Fritto Misto di Pesce*

This light batter creates a golden, crisp coating for any fish. My mom also uses this batter to coat shrimp or calamari. This is a great recipe for fish and chips anytime of the year.

6 cups (1.5 L) canola oil
1 cup (250 mL) all-purpose flour
2 tsp (10 mL) baking powder
½ tsp (2 mL) salt
½ tsp (2 mL) lemon zest
Pinch of pepper
1 cup (250 mL) water

2 lb (1 kg) fish fillets, such as cod, tilapia
  or haddock
1 lb (450 g) small calamari (squid), cleaned
1 lb (450 g) large raw shrimp, peeled
  and deveined
8–10 lemon wedges

IN A DEEP FRYER OR LARGE DEEP SAUCEPAN heat oil to 375°F (190°C).

In a bowl, whisk together flour, baking powder, salt, lemon zest and pepper. Whisk in water until smooth; set aside.

Cut cod into 3-inch (8 cm) chunks. Cut any tentacles off calamari and discard. Cut the calamari into smaller pieces if they are large. Pat shrimp, cod and calamari dry with paper towel.

Dip each fish fillet into batter, letting excess drip back into bowl. Place a few pieces at a time into deep fryer and fry for about 3 minutes or until golden, turning once. Remove with slotted spoon onto paper towel-lined baking sheet. Repeat with remaining fish and seafood. Serve with lemon wedges.

MAKES 8 TO 10 SERVINGS.

You can keep the fish warm in a 250°F (120°C) oven for up to 30 minutes.

Tiramisu Trifle *Zuppa Inglese di Tiramisu*

When you want a twist on traditional tiramisu, this recipe is the one for you. It brings together two different cultures; the famous British trifle and the Italian tiramisu, creating a wonderful recipe. With trifle being a holiday dessert, the Italian twist works perfectly. This is everyone's favourite dessert during holiday time! Not using mascarpone in the cream mixture cuts down the cost, but don't worry, it definitely does not cut down on the flavour.

2 cups (500 mL) 35% whipping cream
1½ cups (375 mL) espresso or strong
  black coffee
⅓ cup (80 mL) coffee, brandy or nut liqueur
1 pkg (500 g) savoiardi or ladyfinger cookies
4 cups (1 L) fresh raspberries
2 Tbsp (30 mL) unsweetened cocoa powder
1 batch Lemon Cream, just made and warm
  (see recipe p. 197), divided

Savoiardi cookies are Italian ladyfingers that are crisp and have one side coated with sugar. There are 4 smaller cello packages in the large bag package you find at Italian grocers and most large grocery stores. You will have leftover cookies from your package and they are delicious to enjoy simply dunked into your coffee or tea.

IN A LARGE BOWL, whip cream until stiff; set aside.

In a shallow bowl, combine coffee and liqueur. Quickly dip each ladyfinger cookie into coffee mixture and start placing cookies in a trifle bowl. Continue with cookies to cover bottom.

Pour half of the Lemon Cream over top the cookie layer. Spread half of the raspberries and whipped cream over top. Dip more cookies and lay another cookie layer on top of cream.

Spread with remaining Lemon Cream, raspberries and whipped cream. Sprinkle evenly with cocoa. Refrigerate overnight or until cookies are softened.

Cover and refrigerate trifle for up to 2 days.

MAKES 8 TO 10 SERVINGS.

Panettone Bread Pudding *Dolce di Panettone*

Panettone is a fruit-studded sweet bread that is enjoyed by Italians all over the world. It's traditionally served over the holiday season on its own, but here it's used in a warm bread pudding. This is an excellent ending to a meal or a comforting snack on a cold winter's night. Plus, it's an easy way to get rid of all those panettone you get for Christmas! Or better yet, wait until after the holidays and pick them up on sale. It's a great dessert for winter weather. Try it with blueberry sauce or marmalade sauce.

8 cups (2 L) cubed panettone bread
   (about half of a panettone)
¼ cup (60 mL) golden raisins
¼ cup (60 mL) cut mixed citrus peel
   (optional)
5 eggs
3 cups (750 mL) milk
¾ cup (190 mL) granulated sugar
1 Tbsp (15 mL) orange zest
1 tsp (5 mL) vanilla

You can substitute any fruit or egg bread for the panettone.

Orange Marmalade Sauce
½ cup (125 mL) orange marmalade
¼ cup (60 mL) orange juice
2 tsp (10 mL) lemon juice
Pinch of cinnamon

SPRINKLE BREAD IN THE BOTTOM of a greased 10-inch (2.5 L) oval baking dish. Sprinkle raisins and candied orange, if using, over top. Set aside.

In a large bowl, whisk together eggs, milk, sugar, orange zest and vanilla. Pour over bread mixture. Cover and refrigerate for at least 1 hour or overnight.

Preheat oven to 375°F (190°C). Uncover and bake for about 45 minutes or until golden and knife inserted in centre comes out clean.

Orange Marmalade Sauce: In a small saucepan, heat marmalade, orange and lemon juices and cinnamon over medium heat until hot. Serve with pudding.

MAKES 8 TO 10 SERVINGS.

Blueberry Sauce Option

1½ cups (375 mL) fresh or frozen blueberries
¼ cup (60 mL) granulated sugar
¼ cup (60 mL) orange juice
¼ cup (60 mL) lemon juice
1 Tbsp (15 mL) cornstarch
1 Tbsp (15 mL) water

IN A SAUCEPAN, combine blueberries, sugar, orange and lemon juice. Whisk together corn-starch and water; stir in. Bring to a boil and cook for 1 minute or until thickened.

New Year's Eve is not complete without a sweet sparkling wine and panettone. As my dad says, "You can't have one without the other." You need the panettone to absorb the alcohol—what a smart guy! It's too bad panettone only go on sale after the holidays or else we could absorb more alcohol during Christmas.

Scalili *Struffoli*

Lovingly referred to as dog bones in our family, these cookies have always been a big favourite with kids. My favourite part was when my mom let me put the sprinkles on. No matter what, there were always a few left stuck to my hand so I had to eat them. The simple things that matter to a kid never change; my daughter loves to help make and eat these now, too! These are traditionally only made at Christmas and we use red and green sprinkles to celebrate the season.

6 eggs

1½ tsp (7 mL) canola oil

1 tsp (5 mL) vanilla or anise extract

½ tsp (2 mL) baking powder

Pinch of salt

3 cups (750 mL) all-purpose flour
  (approx.), divided

4–6 cups (1–1.5 L) canola oil (for frying)

1 cup (250 mL) liquid honey

2 Tbsp (30 mL) coloured sprinkles
  (optional)

IN A LARGE BOWL, whisk together eggs, oil, vanilla, baking powder and salt until smooth. Stir in 2½ cups (625 mL) flour until a soft, but not sticky, dough forms. (You may need to add more flour.) Scrape dough onto a floured work surface and gently knead for about 10 minutes, adding more flour as needed.

Using a small amount of dough each time, roll into a long ½-inch (1 cm) thin rope. Cut into 2-inch (5 cm) pieces. Snip the ends with scissors and continue with remaining dough.

In a deep fryer or a high sided saucepan, heat oil to 375°F (190°C). Carefully drop pieces a few at a time in oil and cook for about 3 minutes or until light golden and puffed. Remove to a paper towel-lined baking sheet and repeat with remaining pieces.

In a large saucepan, heat half of the honey until warm and very liquid. Stir in half of the scallili until coated then using a slotted spoon remove to a large platter. Top with sprinkles, if desired. Repeat with remaining honey and scalili.

MAKES 100 SCALILI.

Make ahead: If you want to make these ahead of time, freeze them before coating with honey. Then simply warm up the honey and the scalili at the same time and coat as directed above.

Turdilli *Turdiddri*

This is a wine cookie that has a very nice but subtle flavour of wine after it is fried and coated in honey. For longer storage, freeze the cookies before coating them in honey and then warm them up in the hot honey to serve when you need them. They are perfect with a shot of liqueur or espresso after your holiday meal. Turdilli is pictured on page 67.

½ cup (125 mL) red wine
¼ cup (60 mL) extra virgin olive oil
1 Tbsp (15 mL) granulated sugar
1 tsp (5 mL) vegetable shortening
1¼ cups (310 mL) all-purpose flour (approx.)
4–6 cups (1–1.5 L) canola oil (for frying)
⅓ cup (80 mL) liquid honey
1–2 Tbsp (15–30 mL) colourful cake sprinkles
  (optional)

I did do a little experiment in my own kitchen and if you don't want to use wine you can use cranberry or grape juice instead. It works well, but the cookies end up a lighter colour when you fry them.

IN A SMALL SAUCEPAN, bring wine, oil, sugar and shortening to a boil. Remove from heat and gradually stir enough of the flour into the mixture to make a soft dough. Dump dough onto a floured surface and let cool until easy enough to handle. Knead remaining flour into the dough, adding up to 2 Tbsp (30 mL) more flour, if needed, to create a soft, supple, smooth dough.

Cut dough into 4 pieces and roll each piece into 10-inch (25 cm) long rope. Cut into 1-inch (2.5 cm) pieces. Roll each piece on the back of a fork or on a gnocchi paddle to create ridges on 1 side and an indent on the other side. Set aside and repeat with remaining dough.

Use a deep fry thermometer in the oil, if using a saucepan, and try to keep it at the temperature range of 325–350°F (160–180°C).

In a deep fryer or a high sided saucepan, heat oil to 325–350°F (160–180°C). Fry about 4–6 turdilli at a time, turning over occasionally for about 3 minutes or until golden brown. Remove with slotted spoon onto paper towel-lined plate. Repeat with remaining cookies.

In a microwaveable bowl, heat honey on high for about 40 seconds or until bubbly. Place cookies into a bowl and pour honey over top and swirl bowl for honey to coat cookies evenly. Place on a platter and sprinkle with cake sprinkles, if desired.

MAKES 40 COOKIES.

Raisin Doughnuts *Castagnole*

I remember watching over the fryer when I was around 6 or 7 with my Nonna as she made big batches of these doughnuts around the holidays. It sat precariously on the fireplace hearth so we could keep an eye on it. The adults always enjoyed them *con gusto* ("with gusto") with coffee, sweet liqueurs or wine.

1 cup (250 mL) golden raisins

1¾ cups (425 mL) all-purpose flour
  (approx.), divided

2 eggs

½ cup (125 mL) granulated sugar

¾ cup (190 mL) milk

3 Tbsp (45 mL) rum

1½ tsp (7 mL) baking powder

1 tsp (5 mL) lemon zest

½ tsp (2 mL) vanilla

Pinch of salt

4–6 cups (1–1.5 L) canola oil for frying

3 Tbsp (45 mL) icing or granulated
  sugar

SOAK RAISINS IN WARM WATER for 10 minutes. Drain well and pat dry. Toss with 2 Tbsp (30 mL) of flour; set aside.

In a large bowl, whisk together eggs and sugar until light coloured. Whisk in milk, rum, baking powder, lemon zest, vanilla and salt until smooth and combined.

Using a wooden spoon, stir in remaining flour and raisins until dough is firm and not too sticky. (If dough is very sticky add a few more tablespoons of flour).

In a deep fryer or large heavy pot half filled with oil and using a deep fry thermometer, heat oil to about 365°F (185°C). Drop batter by teaspoonfuls into hot oil to form balls. Cook for about 5 minutes or until golden brown. Remove to a paper towel-lined baking sheet and repeat with remaining batter.

Place doughnuts in a large bowl and sprinkle with sugar. Toss to coat evenly and serve. Best served warm.

MAKES 40 DOUGHNUTS.

Christmas Biscotti *Biscotti di Natale*

In my family, celebrating Christmas begins early with lots of baking and get-togethers. We also have a cookie exchange each year where I invite family and friends and we end up with many cookies to taste and enjoy. Biscotti are a wonderful addition as they can be made ahead with lots of different flavours. This one highlights the colours of Christmas and aniseed adds a distinct sweet licorice flavour.

1½ cups (325 mL) all-purpose flour
½ tsp (2 mL) baking soda
½ tsp (2 mL) anise seeds, crushed
¼ cup (60 mL) red candied cherries, chopped
¼ cup (60 mL) green candied cherries, chopped

2 eggs
⅓ cup (80 mL) sugar
1 tsp (5 mL) vanilla
1 egg white, beaten
2 tsp (10 mL) coarse sugar

PREHEAT OVEN TO 350°F (180°C). Line baking sheet with parchment paper; set aside.

In a large bowl, combine flour, baking soda and aniseed; stir in red and green cherries.

In another bowl, whisk together eggs, sugar and vanilla; stir into flour mixture until a soft sticky dough forms.

With floured hands, transfer to lightly floured surface; divide in half. Place on prepared baking sheet and shape dough into two 9 × 3-inch (22 × 7 cm) rectangles. Brush with egg white and sprinkle with sugar.

Bake for about 15 minutes or until light golden. Remove from oven and let cool for about 10 minutes. Transfer to cutting board and cut diagonally into ½-inch (1 cm) thick slices. Reduce oven temperature to 300°F (150°C).

Stand slices upright on baking sheet and bake for about 20 minutes or until golden and dry. Let cool on rack.

MAKES 2 DOZEN BISCOTTI.

Store in an airtight container for up to 2 weeks or freeze for up to 2 months.

Ugly but Good Cookies *Biscotti Brutti ma Buoni*

"Ugly but good" is the translation of the name for these crunchy-on-the outside and chewy-on-the-inside Italian cookies. You can make them with coarsely chopped toasted almonds, hazelnuts or walnuts, but they are even more addictive when chunks of chocolate are used instead.

4 egg whites

1 cup (250 mL) sugar

3 Tbsp (45 mL) all-purpose flour

1 tsp (5 mL) vanilla

2 cups (500 mL) coarsely chopped nougat milk chocolate bar (such as Toblerone)

2 Tbsp (30 mL) icing sugar

PREHEAT OVEN TO 350°F (180°C). Line baking sheets with parchment paper; set aside.

In a large heatproof bowl over a saucepan of gently simmering water, whisk together egg whites and sugar. Cook, whisking often, for about 5 minutes or until hot, opaque and sugar is completely dissolved; remove from heat.

In a stand mixer, using whisk attachment, beat mixture for about 7 minutes or until thick and glossy and bowl is cool to the touch. Fold in flour, vanilla and chocolate.

Using a small ice cream scoop, or level tablespoon (15 mL) drop batter onto prepared sheets. Bake, 1 sheet at a time for about 15 minutes or until very golden and firm to the touch. Repeat with remaining batter. Let cool completely in pan on rack. Sprinkle with icing sugar.

MAKES 60 COOKIES.

Make ahead: Store in airtight container for up to 3 days.

Ginger Brutti ma Buoni: Omit vanilla and chocolate. Replace with 1 tsp (5 mL) ground ginger and 1 cup (250 mL) chopped crystallized ginger.

ANTIPASTI

Family gatherings are all about the food and having small bites to share with friends and family is essential. A starter course of appetizers at the table means we will sit longer and enjoy the company.

Spizzici ("small bites") is how we describe the nibbles on the table and our policy is the more, the merrier. Antipasti, which is the plural form of antipasto, simply means starters. This is the Italian way to start any party. These little bites, whether served hot or cold, are meant to stimulate your appetite without filling your tummy, although you might discover that you can easily enjoy a meal of antipasti. This cultural tradition has become very familiar to many people that aren't of Italian decent. I have many friends that serve up melon wrapped in prosciutto and marinated olives or mushrooms because they love all of the different flavours and textures of antipasti.

Along with salty meats and cheeses, we like to serve simple raw vegetables alongside various pickled, roasted and marinated vegetables. But it's the unhurried feeling that accompanies having antipasto before your meal that I really love. It's a time to whet your appetite, enjoy good conversation and try a variety of different foods (and find out about what else will be served later in the meal!).

The best part about sharing food is the planning that goes into it. My family usually talks about the food before we discuss who we are going to invite. When I had children, I was happy thinking about the many birthday parties that we could celebrate with family. Sitting around a table filled with small bites like homemade salami and cheese while sharing stories about what happened in the past year as the birthday person is celebrated is one of my favourite things.

Antipasto Platter *Piatto di Antipasti*

At any Italian deli or grocery store you will notice a vast array of ingredients that are perfect for an antipasto platter. Many of them you can simply purchase and bring home with little preparation; opening a jar and draining some liquid is all that's needed to serve it.

For salamis and other cured meats such as prosciutto, pancetta, sopressata and capicollo, ask for thin slices. The flavour and texture of these cured meats is best enjoyed this way.

A combination of fresh and pickled vegetables can offer up a contrast of flavours and is great to enjoy with *apperitivos* ("before dinner drinks").

You can pick up other little special touches like walnuts, dried figs or fresh grapes to add to the platter to offer a contrast of colours and textures.

Using different cutting boards or serving platters also helps showcase the variety available to your guests and makes it easier to pair up ingredients that you like the flavour of together. Have a variety of breads to serve alongside as well, like Basic Crostini (see recipe p. 82), Taralli (see recipe p. 106) or Fresine Piccolini (see recipe p. 101).

FOR A DELICIOUS ANTIPASTO PLATTER for 12 to 16 people, arrange the following:

8 oz (225 g) thinly sliced prosciutto

4 oz (125 g) thinly sliced hot or mild salami

4 oz (125 g) thinly sliced pancetta

4 oz (125 g) thinly sliced sopressata or capiccollo (hot or mild)

1 batch of Spiced Olives (see recipe p. 80)

1 pint (500 mL) grape or cherry tomatoes

1 batch of Roasted Red Peppers, sliced (see recipe p. 26)

1 cup (250 mL) Pickled Zucchini and Carrots or Pickled Eggplant (see recipes p. 77 or 78)

Half a round of firm ricotta cheese (tuma), cut in wedges or 1 batch of Extra Creamy Ricotta Cheese (see recipe p. 29), drizzled with buckwheat or chestnut honey

A wedge of fresh Parmesan cheese

Pickled Zucchini and Carrots

Giardiniera di Zucchini e Carote

This is just one of the best ways to enjoy vegetables in season. I love the zing the vinegar gives these veggies. If you want them to be a bit less tart, add an additional ½ cup (125 mL) of water to the vinegar before combining with the zucchini and carrots.

My Nonna grates the vegetables so fine they are like cappelini (angel hair pasta). When I make my version they are a bit more rustic and thicker but still delicious.

2 lb (1 kg) small zucchinis (about 5)
12 oz (375 g) carrots, peeled (about 2 large)
¼ cup (60 mL) salt
2 cups (500 mL) white vinegar
3 cloves garlic, minced
1 Tbsp (15 mL) finely chopped fresh parsley
½ tsp (2 mL) hot pepper flakes
½–1 cup (125–250 mL) canola oil

If zucchini are large, be sure to remove the seeds.

TRIM THE ENDS FROM ZUCCHINIS and carrots. Slice both lengthwise and then slice into thin julienne strips. Place strips in a non-reactive colander and sprinkle with salt and toss to coat. Place colander in a large bowl. Cover with paper towels and refrigerate for 12 hours. Rinse well and pat dry with a clean tea towel or paper towels.

Combine vinegar with zucchinis and carrots into a large non-reactive bowl. Cover and refrigerate for 12 hours or for up to 24 hours. Remove from vinegar and squeeze out liquid. Place in a large bowl. Stir in garlic, parsley and hot pepper flakes. Pack into small clean canning jars and pour in enough oil making sure it just covers the top. Place lid on and store in refrigerator for at least 1 day or up to 6 months.

MAKES TWO 2-CUP (500 ML) JARS.

Pickled Eggplant *Melanzane Sott'aceto*

When I want a quick sandwich with plenty of flavour, I reach for this yummy pickled eggplant mix. After pickling it is soft enough to spread. If you spread this onto a fresh crusty bun with fresh ricotta cheese, it makes for an awesome lunch. Or add it to a veal cutlet sandwich for a flavour sensation you won't soon forget. Look for firm eggplants that are heavy for their size for best results and flavour.

2 lb (1 kg) small eggplants (about 2 small or 1 large)
¼ cup (60 mL) salt
2 cups (500 mL) white vinegar
1 cup (250 mL) water

1 Tbsp (15 mL) chopped fresh parsley
2 cloves garlic, minced
½ tsp (2 mL) hot pepper flakes
½–1 cup (125–250 mL) canola oil

PEEL EGGPLANTS and trim ends. Slice eggplants into thin slices and then into thin strips. Place eggplant strips in a colander and sprinkle with salt. Place colander in a large bowl. Using a pot lid or something flat, cover the eggplant strips and weigh it down. Refrigerate for 12 hours.

Rinse the salt from the eggplant and bring vinegar and water to a boil. Add eggplant and boil for 2 minutes. Drain well by pressing eggplant in the strainer to remove excess moisture. Pat dry with a clean tea towel.

In a bowl, combine eggplant with parsley, garlic and hot pepper flakes. Toss with 2 Tbsp (30 mL) of oil and pack into clean canning jars. Add a bit more oil on top to cover the eggplant. Cover with lid. Keep refrigerated for up to 6 months.

MAKES TWO 2-CUP (500 ML) JARS.

Mascarpone Gorgonzola Dip

Salsa al Marscapone e Gorgonzola

These cheeses are not often seen in Southern Italy, but this has become a favourite to serve at family gatherings and in the cooking classes I teach. My favourite way to serve this dip is with fresh fennel slices and celery. Green beans, asparagus and other veggies are also well suited for this dip. Any leftovers are perfect warmed and tossed with hot pasta the next day. A real two in one recipe.

½ cup (125 mL) mascarpone or
   cream cheese
½ cup (125 mL) Gorgonzola cheese
   (about 3 oz / 90 g)

⅓ cup (80 mL) 35% whipping cream
Salt, to taste
Pepper, to taste
Vegetables

IN A FOOD PROCESSOR, pulse together mascarpone, Gorgonzola and whipping cream until smooth. Season with salt and pepper to taste.

Scrape into serving bowl. Serve with vegetables for dipping.

MAKES 1 CUP (250 ML).

> For a chunkier version of the dip simply let all ingredients rest until they are room temperature and stir them together instead of using a food processor. You'll enjoy bits of Gorgonzola in each bite.

Spiced Olives *Olive Aromatiche*

Letting these olives marinate is important because it gives them a flavour boost. Normally served cold or at room temperature, by simply warming them you can bring out the flavours more strongly. Warm olives offer up their juicy interior and salty sweet taste in a way that my family and friends love. If time is of the essence you can always pick some olives up at your favourite deli instead of infusing them with your own flavours. Just warm them up before serving.

1 cup (250 mL) oil-cured black olives
1 cup (250 mL) green olives
½ cup (125 mL) extra virgin olive oil
2 sprigs fresh rosemary

2 sprigs fresh thyme
Pinch of hot pepper flakes
1 strip lemon rind

IN A SMALL SAUCEPAN, heat olives, oil, herbs, hot pepper flakes and lemon rind over medium heat until heated through; the olives should be fragrant and plumped up slightly.

You need to let the olives cool a bit before serving them as they are very hot inside. About 10 or 15 minutes after they are heated through should be enough time.

Serve warm or cover and refrigerate for at least 4 hours or up to 1 week. Let olives come to room temperature before serving after being refrigerated.

MAKES 2 CUPS (500 ML).

> Leaving the herbs and lemon rind in the olives helps deepen the flavour and is a wonderful garnish when serving the olives.

Crostini *Crostini*

Crostini are very versatile. There are seemingly infinite different toppings you can put on them. I like to cook these until they are lightly golden and still a bit soft in the centre; makes it easier to bite into it and not have it shatter. It's never a good thing to have your food all over the front of your shirt. My Zias would surely ask me to take my messy shirt off to wash it for me!

Half a baguette, sliced into about ½-inch (1 cm) thick slices
2 Tbsp (30 mL) extra virgin olive oil

¼ tsp (1 mL) salt
¼ tsp (1 mL) fresh ground pepper

PREHEAT OVEN TO 400°F (200°C).

Brush baguette slices with oil and place on baking sheet.

Bake for about 5 minutes or until they are light golden. Sprinkle with salt and pepper.

MAKES ABOUT 20 CROSTINI.

Wilted Spinach and Garlic Crostini

Spinaci Saltati e Crostini all'Aglio

Deep earthy green spinach with lots of garlic sits atop a toasted baguette slice for the perfect contrast of crunch and softness. For an added flavour hit, place a shaving of aged Parmigiano cheese on top of the spinach before serving.

2 tubs (11 oz / 330 g each) baby spinach, rinsed

¼ cup (60 mL) extra virgin olive oil

6 cloves garlic, minced

2 anchovies, minced

½ tsp (2 mL) hot pepper flakes

1 batch Crostini (see recipe p. 82)

Salt, to taste

You will need 32 cups (8 L) of baby spinach for this recipe.

Depending on how salty your anchovies are, you may need less salt. Be sure to taste the spinach and adjust seasoning to your liking. If you don't have anchovies you can use anchovy paste instead. You will need 2 tsp (10 mL).

COOK HALF OF SPINACH in a large non-stick skillet over medium-high heat stirring often for 5 minutes or until wilted. Place in colander and drain well. Repeat with remaining spinach. Set aside.

Heat the olive oil in skillet over medium heat. Cook garlic, anchovies and hot pepper flakes for about 2 minutes or until just starting to become golden. Add spinach and toss to coat with oil and garlic mixture. Cook for another 2 minutes or until well coated and warmed through. Remove from heat and season to taste with salt.

Divide mixture among crostini and serve.

MAKES 20 CROSTINI.

Ricotta and Roasted Red Pepper Crostini

Crostini con Ricotta e Peperoni Rossi Arrostiti

This is an easy appetizer that I've made for years. Creamy ricotta cheese provides the background for sweet roasted red peppers. Add some peppery arugula for a different flavour and a salute to the Italian flag—highlighting red, white and green. The toppings work beautifully with traditional crostini or with pan-fried polenta (see note below) for gluten-intolerant friends and family.

1 batch Crostini, still warm (see recipe p. 82)
1 clove garlic, cut in half lengthwise
1½ cups (375 mL) thinly sliced Roasted Red Peppers (see recipe p. 26)
1 small clove garlic, minced
2 Tbsp (30 mL) chopped fresh Italian parsley

2 Tbsp (30 mL) extra virgin olive oil
1 Tbsp (15 mL) red wine vinegar
¼ tsp (1 mL) salt
¼ tsp (1 mL) fresh ground pepper
1 cup (250 mL) ricotta cheese
Fresh small basil leaves (optional)

WHILE CROSTINI ARE STILL WARM, rub garlic over baguette slices. Set aside.

In a bowl, combine peppers, garlic, parsley, oil, vinegar, salt and pepper.

Spread ricotta over toasted crostini. Top with peppers and garnish with basil, if using.

MAKES 20 PIECES.

Gluten Free Option: I served this recipe on polenta circles at a friend's gathering who is gluten-free. They loved it! Use a tube of store-bought polenta, slice and pan-fry in oil; top with the ricotta and peppers. So easy.

Mortadella Mousse and Antipasto Crostini

Mousse di Mortadella e Crostini con Antipasto

I grew up asking for San Danielle mortadella, a well recognized brand when I went to the deli with my Nonni or parents. The server would sneak a little slice to me so I could enjoy it while waiting in line on Saturday mornings; such a small gesture that made my day. I brought mortadella to school for lunches, sometimes on a panino (bun), but also on toast bread (that is what we called sliced white bread). I always wanted to change things up and have something that some of the other kids had like peanut butter and jelly. Looking back on it now, I long for those sandwiches and realize how lucky I was to have them.

I love mortadella in sandwiches but I wanted to try something different. I came up with this unique crostini topping, inspired by one of the many Italian magazines I often look through. It combines all the tasty flavours of an antipasto platter on a crostini.

1 Tbsp (15 mL) extra virgin olive oil

2 Tbsp (30 mL) finely chopped roasted
   red peppers

2 Tbsp (30 mL) slivered oil-cured black olives

1 Tbsp (15 mL) small capers

6 oz (180 g) thinly sliced mortadella

⅓ cup (80 mL) unsalted butter, softened

3 Tbsp (45 mL) 35% whipping cream

3 Tbsp (45 mL) chopped fresh Italian parsley

½ tsp (2 mL) fennel seeds, crushed (optional)

1 batch Crostini (see recipe p. 82)

You can use a scant 1/3 cup (80 mL) of jarred antipasto in place of the peppers, olives and capers in the recipe.

IN SMALL BOWL, combine oil, peppers, olives and capers; set aside.

In food processor, blend mortadella, butter and whipping cream until smooth and fluffy. Pulse in parsley and fennel seeds, if using. Scrape into piping bag fitted with star tip. Pipe mousse onto crostini and top with pepper mixture.

MAKES 20 PIECES.

Balsamic Roasted Pear Wedges with Prosciutto

Fette di Pere Arrostite al Balsamico con Prosciutto

We had a pear tree that offered up the most delicious Bartlett pears I have ever tasted. Sometimes I think that the birds and bees enjoy the sweetness of this fruit more than we do! This is a delicious appetizer for entertaining, but it can also be served as a savoury dessert to finish the meal. Serve it with a sparkling wine to start your meal or a sweet ice wine to end your meal. Balsamic vinegar enhances the sweet pear and adds a zip to balance the salty prosciutto.

Gorgonzola Cream Dip

3 oz (90 g) Gorgonzola cheese, at room temperature

¼ cup (60 mL) 35% whipping cream

1 Tbsp (15 mL) chopped fresh Italian parsley

4 firm ripe Bosc or Bartlett pears

¼ cup (60 mL) aged balsamic vinegar

1 Tbsp (15 mL) chopped fresh Italian parsley

1 tsp (5 mL) chopped fresh thyme

1 tsp (5 mL) Dijon mustard

1 clove garlic, minced

Pinch of pepper

12 slices thinly sliced prosciutto, halved lengthwise

Gorgonzola Cream Dip: Stir together Gorgonzola, cream and parsley until smooth; set aside.

PREHEAT OVEN TO 400°F (200°C). Line baking sheet with parchment paper; set aside.

Cut pears in half and remove seeds and core. Cut each half into thirds and set aside.

In a large bowl, whisk together balsamic, parsley, thyme, mustard, garlic and pepper. Add pear wedges and stir to coat well. Let stand for 10 minutes, stirring occasionally.

Remove 1 pear wedge at a time, reserving marinade and wrap with prosciutto slice; place on prepared baking sheet. Repeat with remaining pears and prosciutto. Roast in centre of oven for about 15 minutes or until golden and pears are tender but firm. Spoon remaining marinade over the pears and let cool slightly.

Serve with Gorgonzola Cream Dip.

MAKES 24 PIECES.

Cheese-Filled Rice Balls *Arancini*

These gooey appetizer bites are delicious warm or cold as a snack to watch the game or enjoy with a glass of wine. They are called *arancini,* which means "little oranges" because they have the same colour and shape of the fruit. I have had many variations of this rice ball and you can make up your own fillings with leftovers from your fridge. You will be surprised at what you come up with.

Filling
2½ cups (625 mL) water
1 tsp (5 mL) saffron threads
1½ cups (375 mL) Arborio rice
½ cup (125 mL) freshly grated Romano cheese
2 Tbsp (30 mL) butter
1 egg

Coating
6 oz (180 g) mozzarella, provolone, Asiago or havarti cheese
2 eggs
¼ cup (60 mL) all-purpose flour
1 cup (250 mL) dry seasoned bread crumbs

4–6 cups (1–1.5 L) canola oil (for deep-frying)

Filling: In a large saucepan, bring water and saffron to boil. Add rice; reduce heat to low and cook, stirring frequently, for about 20 minutes or until tender but firm. Add cheese and butter. Let cool completely. Stir in egg; set aside.

Coating: Meanwhile, cut cheese into 16–18 small cubes; set aside.

In a shallow dish, whisk eggs; set aside. Divide rice mixture into 16–18 balls.

With fingers make indentation into each ball and fill with a cheese cube. Seal indentation. Roll balls in flour; then in egg; then in bread crumbs. Set aside on a parchment paper–lined baking sheet.

In large deep saucepan or deep fryer, heat oil over medium heat to 375°F (190°C). Fry balls, in batches, about 2–3 minutes or until golden and crispy.

Drain on a paper towel-lined baking sheet.

MAKES 16 TO 18 BALLS.

Make ahead: You can make the *arancini* up to the point of frying them; cover and refrigerate for up to 4 hours. Let come to room temperature before frying in oil.

PIZZA E PANE

Pane fatta al casa ("homemade bread") truly is a special thing to enjoy. I remember the smell of yeast starting to do its job and, later, the aroma of bread tunneling out of the oven as the loaves my Nonna would bring the loaves out to cool. She wouldn't make just a few loaves. It seemed like a never ending row of buns, loaves and pizzas. It seemed like she was going to feed the whole neighbourhood and in many ways she did. Everyone would stop in after work and we most certainly had to dig into the bread, slathering butter over the top or sneaking over to the pot of bubbling pasta sauce to try whatever Nonna was making.

As a young child, I remember seeing my Nonna dumping out the huge bag of flour onto the dining room table. She would add the yeast to water and start bringing the dough together. This little woman would create the biggest batch of dough I had ever seen. Why the dining room table? It was lower than the counter so she could knead the dough more easily. She would let me knead my own ball of dough and make a small bun, loaf or pizza. I love doing this with my own children now and I hope that it continues as a wonderful Italian tradition for generations to come.

My aunts make amazing bread, too—it seems that generosity is a family trait. We would get a call to come and pick up a few loaves to share it with the family. One call I'll always remember was when Zia Lina, my dad's middle sister, would make *cialetta*, a fresh bread loaf sliced in the middle, liberally drizzled with olive oil, garlic and oregano. She would sandwich the two halves together, wrap in foil and warm it in the oven. Sometimes she sneaks in anchovies for my dad, but he is her baby brother and she likes to spoil him!

I love how all of my family and friends share their love to bread and pizza. My family LOVES pizza. I think it has to do with the flavour, but also the sense of togetherness that eating as a group can bring. It's fun to change up the flavours, an added bonus about this great Italian addition to the world. Whether on its own, alongside antipasti, stirred into soup, added to salads or left to dry for later, bread is something that everyone can enjoy.

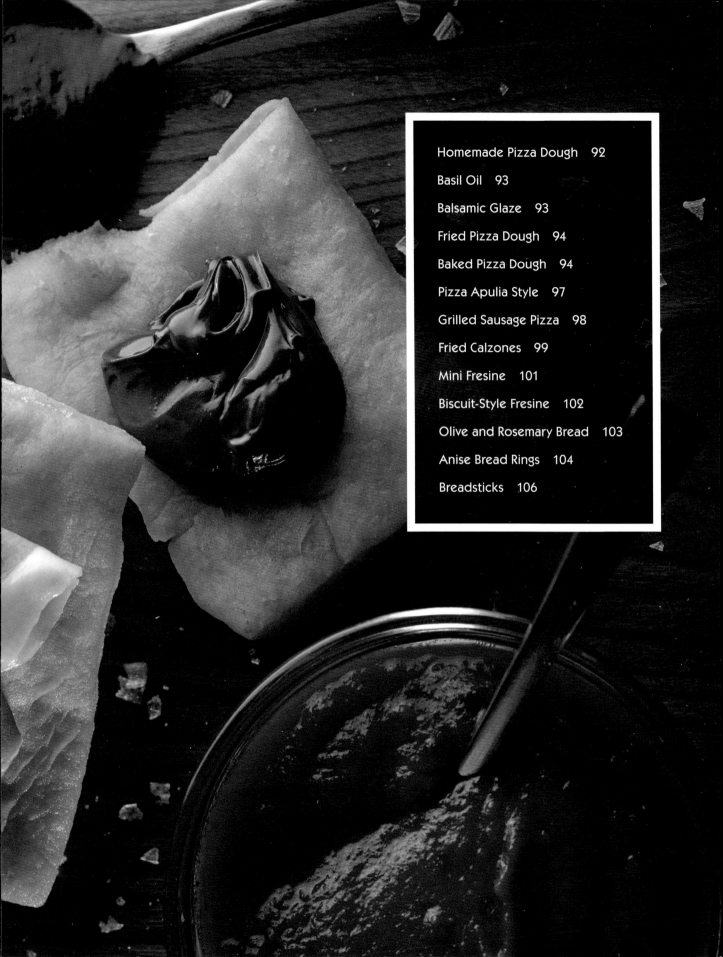

Homemade Pizza Dough

Impasto per la Pizza Fatta in Casa

I love making pizza. It's super fun when the kids help out and make their own; it can easily become a party. This carries on my Nonna's tradition. She would make sheets and sheets of pizza and then invite everyone over to enjoy it for dinner. When we were lucky and there were leftovers, she would wrap them in foil, ready to pop into the oven the next day for lunch. Some of my favourite toppings were leftover meatballs and sausages from pasta sauce or mushrooms and peppers that she had cooked in a bit of oil. But the best part was there was never a crust to the pizza she made. She would always place toppings right to the edge, making sure every piece was covered with delicious goodness. I worked on creating this dough for a long time; it had to be easy to work with and have the same crisp crust that I enjoyed in Italy, similar to my Nonna's. Make lots and freeze it to use later. You can double or triple it easily for big crowds.

Pinch of sugar
⅔ cup (150 mL) warm water
1 envelope (8 g) active dry yeast
2 Tbsp (25 mL) extra virgin olive oil
¼ tsp (1 mL) salt
1½ cups (375 mL) all-purpose flour

2 1/4 tsp (11 mL) is equivalent to one envelope of yeast. I use my yeast often so I buy a jar and keep it in the pantry but if you don't use yours often, be sure to keep it in the refrigerator for added freshness. It may take a bit longer to activate when it's cold.

IN A LARGE BOWL, dissolve sugar into water. Sprinkle with yeast and let stand for about 10 minutes or until frothy. Whisk in olive oil and salt. Add flour and scrape out onto floured surface. Knead gently just until smooth dough forms. Place in a greased bowl and cover with plastic wrap; let stand for about 1 hour or until doubled in bulk.

Press out to size of a pizza crust and use right away.

MAKES ONE 14-INCH (28 CM) PIZZA.

Make ahead: After kneading the dough, place in a greased reasealable bag and refrigerate for up to 1 day or freeze for up to 2 weeks. From refrigerator, let come to room temperature before using. If frozen, thaw in refrigerator overnight before thawing at room temperature.

HERE ARE A COUPLE TREATS to drizzle over your pizza when serving or simply to have as a dip with bread. I also use both of them to garnish plates when serving. So easy to make and delicious, too. I think you will agree!

Basil Oil *Olio di Basilico*

This oil has a rich green colour and is easy to use for plate garnishes, salads, pizzas and pastas. You can use it for salad dressings, too.

1 cup (250 mL) extra virgin olive oil
1 cup (250 mL) packed fresh basil leaves

PUREE OIL AND BASIL in blender or food processor until smooth. I like leaving the leaves in for extra basil flavour. It will darken as it sits. Cover and refrigerate for up to 2 weeks.

MAKES 1 CUP (250 ML).

Balsamic Glaze *Glassa Balsamica*

Here's a great trick to make less expensive balsamic vinegar taste like a slightly aged, more expensive one. This is great for salad dressings, garnishing or drizzling over grilled meats and pizzas.

1 cup (250 mL) balsamic vinegar
¼ cup (60 mL) packed brown sugar

IN A SMALL SAUCEPAN, bring vinegar and brown sugar to boil, stirring constantly. Reduce heat and simmer for about 3 minutes or until slightly syrupy.

MAKES 1 CUP (250 ML).

Fried Pizza Dough *Impasto Fritto*

If you don't want to make your dough you can pick some up at the deli or grocery store. Either way, you have to try this tasty treat when you have friends over for pizza. You can even save some and serve it up for dessert by spreading it with a little Nutella or a smear of ricotta with shaved chocolate and strawberries. Mamma mia, this is good stuff!

2 batches Homemade Pizza Dough
   (see recipe p. 92) or 1 bag (750 g)
   storebought pizza dough

½ cup (125 mL) extra virgin
   olive oil

CUT DOUGH IN HALF; refrigerate half. Lightly flour work surface and roll out pizza dough to a very thin 12-inch (30 cm) square, making sure to let the dough rest in between rolling. Using a pizza cutter, cut into 16 squares.

   Meanwhile, in a large non-stick skillet, heat oil over medium-high heat. Place a few pieces of the dough into oil and let cook for about 2 minutes or until starting to bubble and become golden. Turn dough over and cook until golden. Remove to paper towel-lined platter and repeat with remaining dough. Turn down the heat as necessary so dough doesn't burn. Sprinkle with salt if desired and enjoy with prosciutto or other fine Italian deli meats and cheeses. Repeat with refrigerated dough.

MAKES 32 PIECES.

Baked Pizza Dough *Impasto Cotto al Forno*

2 batches Homemade Pizza Dough
   (see recipe p. 92) or 1 bag (750 g)
   storebought pizza dough
2 Tbsp (30 mL) extra virgin olive oil

1 Tbsp (15 mL) grated Parmigiano
   Reggiano cheese
1 tsp (5 mL) dried oregano leaves

PREHEAT OVEN TO 425°F (220°C). Grease 2 baking sheets with oil; set aside.

   Cut dough in half; refrigerate half. Lightly flour work surface and roll out pizza dough to a very thin 12-inch (30 cm) square, making sure to let the dough rest in between rolling.

   Brush dough with oil and sprinkle with cheese and oregano. Using a pizza cutter, cut into 16 squares. Place on greased baking sheets and bake for about 10 minutes or until puffed and golden.

   Repeat with refrigerated dough.

MAKES 32 PIECES.

Pizza Apulia Style *Pizza Pugliese*

Simplicity is key when it comes to many Italian meals. Apulia is on the Eastern coast of Southern Italy. In the town of Bari, while looking onto the Adriatic Sea, my dad's Zio's family enjoyed the calmness of the water and living by the beach. They lived a simple life which is showcased in the simple flavours that shine through in this pizza. Puglia is known for its wine and wine has always been a perfect match for pizza. Inspired by that combination, this pizza has a thin, crisp crust with no tomato sauce; just simple ingredients that shine through. It makes me think of family enjoying the sweet life—*la dolce vita*.

1 batch Homemade Pizza Dough
  (see recipe p. 92)
2–4 Tbsp (30–60 mL) extra virgin
  olive oil
2 small onions, very thinly sliced
1 cup (250 mL) fresh shredded Romano
  cheese

1 tsp (5 mL) dried oregano
¼ tsp (1 mL) hot pepper flakes
  (optional)
Salt, to taste (optional)
Fresh ground pepper (optional)

PREHEAT OVEN TO 425°F (220°C).

Punch dough down and knead gently. Stretch the dough to fit a 14-inch (35 cm) round pizza pan.

Brush pizza dough with 2 Tbsp (30 mL) extra virgin olive oil. Sprinkle onions on top evenly. Sprinkle with cheese, oregano and red pepper flakes, if using. Drizzle with 1–2 Tbsp (15–30 mL) more olive oil, if desired. Bake in centre of oven for about 20 minutes or until golden brown.

Season with salt and pepper, if desired.

MAKES 4 TO 6 SERVINGS.

Grilled Sausage Pizza *Pizza con Salsiccia Grigliata*

I like serving up this pizza in the same shape pizzas are served in Italy—long oval. This recipe is designed for cooking the pizza on the grill or barbecue, and you can use different toppings easily. Make the pizza as an appetizer or for your dinner with a crisp green salad.

You can use leftover grilled vegetables with this recipe, such as eggplant or zucchini.

3 Tbsp (45 mL) extra virgin olive oil, divided
1 small red pepper, quartered
1 yellow zucchini, sliced lengthwise
4 oz (110 g) package oyster mushrooms
2 fresh spicy sausages
1 batch Homemade Pizza Dough (see recipe p. 92)
⅓ cup (80 mL) Homemade Tomato Sauce (see recipe p. 23)
1 Tbsp (15 mL) Homemade Pesto Sauce (see recipe p. 122)
1½ cups (375 mL) shredded mozzarella or provolone cheese
1 Tbsp (15 mL) chopped fresh parsley

You will need approximately 2 cups (500 mL) of oyster mushrooms if you buy them in bulk.

PREHEAT GRILL to medium-high heat.

Drizzle half of the oil over red pepper, zucchini and mushrooms. Place sausages and vegetables on greased grill. Close lid and grill, turning frequently, for about 5 minutes for mushrooms, 10 minutes for pepper and zucchini and about 15 minutes for the sausages. Remove from grill; let cool slightly. Slice sausages, pepper and squash on a diagonal and set aside.

Working on a floured surface, cut pizza dough in half and stretch out each half into an oval, about 12 × 14 inches (30 × 35 cm) long. Rub remaining oil over both sides of dough and place on greased grill over medium-high heat and grill, turning once for about 5 minutes or until light golden and firm. Remove to cutting board.

In small bowl, combine pasta sauce and pesto. Spread over both pizza doughs. Spread sausage, pepper, zucchini and mushrooms over both shells. Sprinkle with cheese.

Turn the grill down to low. Place pizzas on grill, close lid and grill for about 10 minutes or until cheese is melted and crust is crispy. Sprinkle with parsley before serving.

MAKES 4 SERVINGS.

Oven Baked Variation: Instead of grilling the pizza, you can stretch out dough and place on a pizza pan to bake in a 400°F (200°C) oven for about 20 minutes or until cheese is melted and crust is crispy.

Fried Calzones *Calzone Fritti*

When you make pizza the family is happy . . . but when you make calzones (also known as panzerotti) the family is ecstatic! You can bake these stuffed pizzas in 400°F (200°C) oven for about 20 minutes or until golden brown but my preference is to fry them up in oil. Put your favourite pizza toppings in them to change the taste.

2 batches Homemade Pizza Dough (see recipe p. 92) or 1 bag (750 g) store-bought pizza dough
1 cup (250 mL) Homemade Tomato Sauce (see recipe p. 23)
1 small clove garlic, minced
½ tsp (2 mL) dried oregano
1 cup (250 mL) sliced pepperoni

1 cup (250 mL) sliced mushrooms
1 green pepper, thinly sliced
1 onion, thinly sliced (optional)
2 cups (500 mL) shredded mozzarella or provolone cheese
1 egg white, lightly beaten
6 cups (1.5 L) canola oil (for frying)

DIVIDE DOUGH INTO 4 EQUAL PARTS and roll each into a 9-inch (4.5 cm) circle. Cover lightly with a clean tea towel and set aside.

In a small bowl, stir together pasta sauce, garlic and oregano. Spread sauce over half of each of the pizza circles. Sprinkle with pepperoni, mushrooms, green pepper and onion, if using. Sprinkle evenly with cheese. Brush edge of pizza dough with egg white and fold dough over filling to form half-moon shape. Pinch edge to seal.

In a deep fryer or a large heavy saucepan heat oil over medium heat to 375°F (190°C). Place 1 calzone at a time in oil and cook, turning once, for about 5 minutes or until golden brown. Remove with tongs onto a paper towel-lined plate and repeat with remaining calzones.

MAKES 4 SERVINGS.

Mini Fresine *Fresine Piccoline*

Making fresh buns is fun but how about drying them out and saving them for later? Yes, it's not a mistake. With this recipe, we make fresh bread only to dry it out for later. It's a great way to always have bread on hand. You can use these as little crackers, keeping them crispy to serve with cheeses or quickly run them under water to serve as bread to eat with antipasto like cheeses or salami. I love adding them dry to salads and soups to sop up liquid and enjoy the contrast of texture they bring. They absorb the flavour of the vinegar in salads and the broth in soups.

3 eggs
⅓ cup (80 mL) canola oil
½ cup (125 mL) warm water
1 tsp (5 mL) sugar
1 Tbsp (15 mL) active dry yeast
3½ cups (875 mL) all-purpose flour (approx.)
1 tsp (5 mL) salt

You can use ⅓ cup (80 mL) of melted butter in place of the canola oil.

IN A BOWL, whisk together eggs and oil.

In a separate large bowl, combine water with sugar and sprinkle with yeast. Let stand for 10 minutes or until frothy. Whisk in egg mixture and stir in flour and salt. Remove dough from bowl onto a floured surface and knead to form a smooth dough, adding more flour if necessary. Place in an oiled bowl; cover and let rise for 1 hour or until doubled in size.

Preheat oven to 350°F (180°C). Line a baking sheet with parchment paper; set aside.

Cut dough into quarters and roll each quarter into long strips and cut into small pieces. Shape each piece into small 1-inch (2.5 cm) balls. Place on baking sheet and bake for about 15 minutes or until light brown. Repeat with remaining dough.

Cut each bun in half and return, cut side up, to baking sheet. Reduce oven temperature to 200°F (95°C). Return cut fresine to oven for about 1 hour or until crisp. Let cool completely.

MAKES 60 FRESINE.

Biscuit-Style Fresine *Fresine Stile Biscotti*

My mom made these fresine a few times and they became a big hit with friends. I think having an almost hard texture on the outside with a slight chewiness on the inside makes these perfect to serve up with cheese instead of crackers. You can also top them with fresh ricotta cheese and sprinkle them with chopped nuts and a drizzle of oil or chestnut honey. Try many different toppings and you may have a new favourite for entertaining at your home, too!

4 cups (1 L) all-purpose flour
5 tsp (20 mL) baking powder
Pinch of salt

2 eggs
⅔ cup (150 mL) canola oil
½ cup (125 mL) water (approx.)

PREHEAT OVEN TO 350°F (180°C). Line a baking sheet with parchment paper; set aside.

In a large bowl, whisk together flour, baking powder and salt. Make a well and, using a fork, beat in eggs, oil and half of the water. Start to bring in the flour to make a dough. If the dough seems a bit dry and crumbly, drizzle in some more of the water.

Bring dough together with your hands and knead gently a few times. Roll out onto a floured surface to about 1 inch (2.5 cm) thick. Using a small cookie cutter or glass, cut out 1½-inch (3 cm) circles and place on prepared baking sheet. Repeat until all dough is used.

Bake in oven for about 15 minutes or until light golden in colour. Cut in half and place back on baking sheet. Return to oven for about 5 minutes or until crisp. Let cool completely.

MAKES 6 DOZEN FRESINE.

Olive and Rosemary Bread *Pane con Olive e Rosmarino*

This bread brings a wonderful aroma to your kitchen and is the perfect addition to serve up with antipasto or your main meal. I also like to bring fresh bread with me when invited over to family and friend's homes, along with a bottle of wine. I learned this from my relatives who are always welcoming with open arms.

½ tsp (2 mL) sugar

1¼ cups (310 mL) warm water

2 tsp (10 mL) active dry yeast

3 Tbsp (45 mL) extra virgin olive oil, divided

3½ cups (875 mL) all-purpose flour (approx.), divided

1 tsp (5 mL) salt

½ cup (125 mL) chopped pitted sundried black olives

1 Tbsp (15 mL) chopped fresh rosemary

Extra virgin olive oil, for brushing

IN A LARGE BOWL, dissolve sugar in warm water. Sprinkle in yeast and let stand for 10 minutes or until frothy. Stir in 2 Tbsp (30 mL) oil. Stir in 3 cups (750 mL) flour and salt to form soft sticky dough. Turn out onto a lightly floured surface. Knead for about 5 minutes, adding more flour if necessary, to form a smooth, elastic dough. Let rest for 5 minutes.

Flatten dough into a disk and sprinkle with olives and rosemary. Fold dough over and knead for about 3 minutes or until olives are evenly distributed (You may need to add some more flour to help prevent the dough from sticking to the counter). Form into a ball. Place dough in greased bowl. Cover and let rise for about 1 hour or until doubled in size.

Turn out dough onto a lightly floured surface. Press down dough into 11 × 8-inch (28 × 20 cm) rectangle. Starting at narrow end, roll the dough up into a cylinder, pinching along bottom to smooth and seal. Fit into greased 8 × 4-inch (20 × 10 cm) loaf pan. Cover and let rise for about 1 hour or until doubled in bulk. Brush top with remaining oil.

Preheat oven to 400°F (200°C).

Bake in centre of oven for about 35 minutes or until golden brown and loaf sounds hollow when tapped on bottom. Remove from pan and let cool before enjoying.

MAKES 1 LOAF.

Focaccia Variation: To make this dough into a focaccia, instead of rolling it into a cylinder, press dough into an 8-inch (20 cm) round baking pan and let rise. Before baking push fingers gently in top to make a few indentations and brush with oil.

Anise Bread Rings *Ciambella d'Anice*

Sharing bread for Italians only makes sense. With a toast of wine and a wonderful meal you surely have an Italian feast in the making, I thought it would be meaningful as a round ring to show the ongoing love Italians have for bread.

I love talking about food. Italian food, of course, is always at the tip of my tongue and sharing recipes seems to happen naturally for me. One weekend when I was away with some girlfriends, one of the staff at the hotel we were at was Italian. We started chatting and she shared her recipe for *ciambella*. She told me everyone makes it differently, which is true, but her recipe is in the style that my dad would drive out of town to get. This recipe has just the right amount of chewiness, and is adapted from Lydia, the woman I met that day.

6 cups (1.5 L) all-purpose flour

1 Tbsp (15 mL) salt

2 tsp (10 mL) anise seeds

1 Tbsp (15 mL) quick rise dry yeast

2 cups (500 mL) warm water, divided

1 Tbsp (15 mL) extra virgin olive oil

IN A LARGE BOWL, combine flour, salt and anise seeds.

In another bowl, combine yeast with ½ cup (125 mL) warm water; let stand for 10 minutes or until frothy. Pour into the flour mixture and add remaining water. Mix together, kneading to form a ball.

Place dough in an oiled bowl and score a cross on top of the dough. Cover with a clean tea towel and let rise for 2 hours.

Bring a large pot of water to boil and add oil.

Punch down dough and cut into 8 equal pieces. Roll each piece of dough out into a long rope. Twist 2 pieces of dough together, and press the ends firmly together to form a circle to join the twisted pieces together.

Preheat oven to 400°F (200°C).

Place one ring in the boiling water; boil for 1 minute or until it comes to the top. (Don't worry if the ring comes apart a little in the water, it will still be delicious.) Flip the ring over and remove it to a clean tea towel. Repeat with remaining dough.

Place dough rings directly on an oven rack in middle of oven. Bake for about 20 minutes or until bottom is light brown and crisp. Turn them over and bake for about 15 minutes more or until golden.

MAKES 4 CIAMBELLA.

Breadsticks *Taralli*

What are *taralli*? If you see them in stores or at home they might be little round circles of hard bread which are great with coffee. In my house, we never called them *taralli*, we called them "viscotti" which I enjoyed (and still enjoy) dipped in coffee. The word is very similar to biscotti and like biscotti, they are cooked twice. First they are boiled in water, then baked in the oven to achieve their crisp texture.

As a kid, to keep me occupied, I was allowed to dip my "viscotti" into one of the adult's coffee. I remember also enjoying a late night snack with my Nonno on the couch while he watched Benny Hill. He would eat a chunk of cheese with some "viscotti," while I enjoyed mine as is.

Now I let my kids do the same. Although Matthew, my oldest son, now enjoys it with his tea and milk.

In my family, when children are teething we give them one to suck on with their gums, but you have to watch them like a hawk in case their gums became strong enough to break a piece off. I was a happy baby, as were my cousins, with one of these in my mouth.

I often serve these now to adults to enjoy with salami, cheese and other appetizers. Just when you need something *a boca* (in your mouth), as my dad says.

Pinch of sugar
1 cup (250 mL) warm water
2 tsp (10 mL) active dry yeast
2 Tbsp (30 mL) canola oil

3 cups (750 mL) all-purpose flour
 (approx.), divided
1½ tsp (7 mL) salt

IN A LARGE BOWL, combine sugar and water. Sprinkle yeast into bowl and let stand for 10 minutes or until frothy. Stir in oil, 2½ cups (625 mL) flour and salt until a ragged dough forms.

Scrape out onto a floured surface and knead until smooth. Place dough in an oiled bowl and turn to coat lightly with oil. Cover lightly with a clean towel and let rise for about 1 hour or until doubled in size.

Punch down dough and knead in remaining flour until a firm, stiff dough forms. Divide dough into 12 pieces and roll each into long thin ropes about 12 inches (30 cm) long. Bring ends together and pinch to seal. Place on a clean tea towel.

Bring a large pot of water to a gentle boil and add *taralli* a few at a time, for about 1 minute, turning once. Using a slotted spoon slid under the *taralli*, pull it up supporting with tongs. Remove from water and place on a clean tea towel and repeat with remaining *taralli*.

Preheat oven to 350°F (180°C).

Place *taralli*, 6 at a time, directly on middle rack in oven (keeping away from the sides of the oven). Bake for about 15 minutes until firm and set. Turn over and bake for another 10 minutes or until light golden and crisp.

Repeat with remaining *taralli*.

MAKES 12 TARALLI.

You can make the taralli any size you want, smaller or larger, and if they don't stay together not to worry, you can do simple sticks instead. Either way, these will last a long time in a bag in your cupboard. Great for a snack anytime.

FIRST COURSES AND LIGHT MEALS

I was lucky to hang out with my maternal Nonna from a very young age while my parents were working. There was no question that I loved my time with her. She would take me grocery shopping, let me help with laundry, play with bread dough and cook meals for Nonno and my family during the day. Summer days were spent outside playing and digging in the garden, gathering up vegetables and fruit for the day's meals. When we weren't outside in the garden, I was inside running around the house with my rolling riding duck or climbing on Nonno's La-Z-Boy with my stuffed monkey. Not a care in the world. What I didn't realize was that it was these times with Nonna that would help mold my future love of family and food.

These days, Nonna still lives in Sault Ste Marie where I grew up. It's an eight hour drive to Northern Ontario from Guelph, where I live now, so when we do get together it's always a big deal. We love it when Nonna comes here to visit because there is always good food and fun to be had. When I started my recipe developing career in the Canadian Living test kitchen in Toronto, Nonna actually came to the test kitchen where I was working and made gnocchi for everyone. It was a blast for everyone who working at the magazine and Nonna, too!

It always brings us great joy when Nonna and Nonno show up. My kids are excited to see them and to enjoy Nonna's food. There are plenty of days that my daughter says, "Can we have Nonna's sauce?"

Nonno plays a big part as well. Questions like, "Did Nonno bring some salami for us?" warm my heart. I hearing this from my kids because through the gifts of food, they realize how much they are loved.

I hope that I can share that experience with my younger relatives' families and I look forward to having that enjoyment when I get older as well. For now, I'm happy to share my memories with my children and continue to build new memories, too.

Pasta Dough *Impasto per la Pasta*

If you have a pasta machine you can make all different shapes and sizes of pasta. I remember helping my Nonna and mom when pasta was being made. We would hang sheets of pasta off of broom handles balanced on the backs of chairs to dry. It was so much fun that I would dance around the pasta sheets as if I was cheering the pasta to dry. Nothing beats a plate of homemade "pastashutta," which is slang for pasta but also an endearing term that my dad has always used when talking to little kids, including my own children!

This dough makes perfect all-purpose pasta for any occasion.

1½ cups (375 mL) all-purpose flour
  (approx.)
3 eggs

1½ tsp (7 mL) salt
1 tsp (5 mL) extra virgin olive oil

MOUND FLOUR ON COUNTER or in a large bowl. Make a well in centre of the flour. In a small bowl, whisk together eggs, salt and oil. Pour into well and begin mixing with fork, incorporating small amounts of flour at a time until a soft dough forms. Turn out onto a floured surface.

Knead dough for about 5 minutes, adding more flour if necessary, until a firm, smooth dough forms. Cover with a tea towel and let rest for about 15 minutes.

Cut dough into 4 equal pieces. Using a pasta machine, roll 1 piece at a time through the thickest, or first, setting two times. Continue through settings until a smooth, thin pasta piece is formed. Lay flat on a floured surface and let dry for about 15–30 minutes. Continue with remaining dough.

For long pasta: Place dough at top of pasta cutter and roll through. Wrap into little nests and let dry completely for long storage or cook immediately.

For lasagne sheets, see Cannelloni recipe p. 135.

MAKES PASTA FOR 4 TO 6 SERVINGS.

Roasted Squash Agnolotti

Agnolotti alla Zucca Arrostita

Agnolotti translated means "Priests' caps" named for the shape of this pasta, a small crescent-shaped ravioli.

My agnolotti contain a delicate sweet squash filling. This is a great recipe for a get-together with friends or family as you can make large batches and then divide the agnolotti up as needed.

6 cups (1.5 L) cubed butternut squash
  (about 1 small squash)
2 Tbsp (30 mL) extra virgin olive oil
1 small head garlic
Pinch of salt
Pinch of pepper
¼ cup (60 mL) whipping cream
2 batches Pasta Dough sheets (see recipe p. 110)
1 egg, beaten

You can look for prepared squash in grocery stores to make this filling quickly with less prep work. You will need about 1.3 lb (600 g).

PREHEAT OVEN TO 425°F (220°C). Line a baking sheet with parchment paper; set aside.

In a large bowl, toss together squash and oil. Place on prepared baking sheet. Trim top of garlic head to expose cloves. Place cut side down on same baking sheet. Roast for about 40 minutes or until squash and garlic are tender and golden brown. Let cool slightly.

Squeeze garlic out of its skin and into a food processor bowl. Add roasted squash, salt and pepper. Pulse to coarsely chop squash. Add cream; puree until smooth to make about 2 cups (500 mL) filling.

Cut 3-inch (7.5 cm) circles using a cookie cutter or ravioli press out of pasta dough sheets. Place a heaping teaspoon of the filling in centre of each circle. Brush outer edge of each circle with some of the egg. Fold dough over to create a half-moon shape; pinch edges together. Place on a floured tea towel on a large baking sheet. Continue with remaining dough and filling. Let agnolotti air dry for about 4 hours, turning occasionally until firm.

In a large pot of boiling salted water, cook agnolotti for about 5 minutes or until they float to the top. Drain and toss with your favourite pasta sauce.

MAKES 50 AGNOLOTTI OR 6 SERVINGS.

Make ahead: Freeze uncooked agnolotti until firm and solid, about 2 hours. Place in a resealable plastic bag and freeze for up to 2 months.

Meat-Filled Ravioli *Ravioli Ripieni di Carne*

I have a collection of fun ravioli presses for pasta that my Nonna gave me. They look like ice cube trays that are filled with pasta and meat or cheese filling. Not to worry if you don't have any of these, ravioli are easy to make and fill. I used to sneak the meat filling in spoonfuls when my Nonna was making them. Now my son does the same but I think his appetite is bigger than mine was! Using this loose meat filling in the ravioli adds a nice touch not found in store-bought pasta.

3 slices pancetta, finely diced

3 cloves garlic, minced

8 oz (225 g) lean ground pork, turkey
  or veal

½ tsp (2 mL) dried oregano leaves

½ tsp (2 mL) salt

½ cup (125 mL) chopped Italian parsley

¼ cup (60 mL) fresh grated Parmesan
  cheese

2 egg yolks

1 batch Pasta Dough sheets (see recipe
  p. 110)

1 egg, beaten

IN A LARGE NON-STICK SKILLET, cook pancetta over medium-high heat for about 1 minute or until fat renders. Add garlic, pork, oregano and salt and cook for about 8 minutes or until the meat is browned. Add parsley and cheese. Let cool slightly. Stir in egg yolks. Let cool completely. The filling should make about 2 cups (500 mL).

> *You can use this filling to make manicotti (meat-filled pasta rolls) and bake them like the Spinach Ricotta Cannelloni recipe. (see recipe p. 135)*

Meanwhile, lightly score squares on each sheet of pasta dough. Place a heaping teaspoon of the filling in the centre of each square. Brush the edges of each square with beaten egg. Top with another sheet of pasta dough. Gently push dough around filling to let air escape, sealing around edges. Continue with remaining dough.

Using a pastry cutter or large knife, cut each square around score lines. Place on floured tea towel on large baking sheet. Continue with remaining dough and filling. Let ravioli air dry for about 4 hours, turning occasionally until firm.

In a large pot of boiling salted water, cook ravioli for about 5 minutes or until they float to the top. Drain and toss with Homemade Tomato Sauce (recipe p. 23).

MAKES 2 DOZEN RAVIOLI.

Make ahead: Freeze uncooked ravioli on baking sheet until firm and solid, about 2 hours. Place in a resealable plastic bag and freeze for up to 2 months.

Potato Gnocchi *Gnocchi di Patate*

These little dumplings were one of the first doughs I placed my hands on. Soft, supple dough that my Nonna let me roll in the little basket (also called a *cestino*) to get the distinctive little lines on them. When it was time to get my own *cestino*, she asked her sister in Aiello, Calabria to send one over. But not directly to me, as my Nonna had to inspect it first to make sure the gnocchi would come out perfectly! I have since gone back to the local market in Aiello and bought many sizes of *cestino* just in case I ever misplace one. I still cherish the one that was given to me; I think it makes the best gnocchi.

You can enjoy these gnocchi as part of a meal or as a meal on their own. Coated with a tomato or meat sauce, they are delicious.

7 yellow-fleshed potatoes, about 2 lb (1 kg)
2 tsp (10 mL) salt
3 cups (750 mL) all-purpose flour (approx.)

Nonna would save her oldest potatoes for gnocchi. The eyes that were growing out of them, seemed to indicate that these potatoes made the best gnocchi. Be sure to remove the eyes though, as they are not edible. You can use any potato you have, but I like to use the giallo (yellow) potato for its colour and flavour. New potatoes tend to give you a slightly gluey texture and a heavier gnocchi.

PEEL AND CUBE potatoes. Place in a large pot and cover with water. Bring to a boil and cook for about 20 minutes or until tender. Drain well; let stand for 5 minutes in strainer.

Put potatoes through a food mill or ricer, in batches, into large bowl. Let cool slightly. Stir in salt. Stir in enough flour to form slightly sticky, soft dough.

Divide dough into 8 pieces. Roll into a long rope about ½ inch (1 cm) thick. Cut into ½-inch (1 cm) pieces. Toss with flour. Roll along fork to form grooves. Toss with flour and place on a floured baking sheet. Repeat with remaining dough. Place in freezer for about 1 hour or until firm.

In a large pot of boiling salted water, add gnocchi in batches and cook for about 3 minutes or until they float. Using a slotted spoon or small sieve, scoop out gnocchi and place in a large bowl. Repeat with remaining gnocchi.

MAKES 2 LB (1 KG), ENOUGH FOR 4 TO 6 SERVINGS.

Potato Gnocchi with Two Sauces

Gnocchi di Patate con due Salse

Every Italian feast includes pasta and one of my favourites is gnocchi. This recipe tosses the gnocchi first in sage butter and then tops it with a tomato sauce.

1 batch Potato Gnocchi (see recipe p. 116),
  divided
6 Tbsp (90 mL) butter, divided
1 small onion, finely chopped
½ tsp (2 mL) salt
¼ tsp (1 mL) pepper
1 can (28 oz / 796 mL) plum tomatoes, crushed
12 fresh sage leaves, chopped, divided
⅔ cup (150 mL) fresh grated Parmesan cheese

You can use 3 cups (750 mL) of canned tomatoes for this recipe.

IN A LARGE DEEP SKILLET, heat 2 Tbsp (30 mL) butter over medium heat. Cook onion, salt and pepper for about 5 minutes or until softened. Add tomatoes and simmer for about 15 minutes or until thickened.

Meanwhile, in a large pot of boiling salted water, add half of the gnocchi and cook for about 4 minutes or until the gnocchi float and are cooked through. Remove with a slotted spoon into a serving bowl. Repeat with remaining gnocchi.

In another large skillet melt another 2 Tbsp (30 mL) butter over medium heat and cook half of the sage leaves for 1 minute. Add half of the gnocchi and toss to coat. Scrape into platter.

Repeat with remaining butter, sage and gnocchi.

Spoon tomato sauce over top of gnocchi and sprinkle with cheese.

MAKES 4 TO 6 SERVINGS.

Spinach Ricotta Gnocchi *Gnocchi di Ricotta e spinaci*

These delicate little dumplings are from Zia Lina, my dad's middle sister. She also makes a plain ricotta version without the spinach that is equally delicious (see the tip p. 120). She makes these for special occassions (usually when we visit!), but they work for any family meal. If you're not a fan of spinach just omit it.

In addition to the gnocchi basket from my Nonna, I also have a gnocchi paddle that makes the ridges on gnocchi perfectly. After showing my dad the little board, he made me my own paddle, just the right size for me! He later made a box full which I take with me to cooking classes to sell. It was such a pleasure to showcase my dad's craft as a woodworker and carpenter. Most of my students were happy to buy one and take it home to recreate gnocchi for their families. It makes me smile knowing people have some of my family's work in their homes.

1 large tub (11 oz / 330 g) baby spinach, washed

You will need about 16 cups (4 L) of lightly packed baby spinach.

1 egg

1 tub (475 g) ricotta cheese

You will need 1 1/2 cups (375 mL) of ricotta cheese.

3 cups (750 mL) all-purpose flour (approx.), divided

½ tsp (2 mL) salt

1 batch of Homemade Tomato (see recipe p. 23) or Easy Gorgonzola sauce (see recipe p. 124)

IN A LARGE SKILLET, cover and cook spinach over medium heat for about 5 minutes. Drain and squeeze spinach well. Chop spinach; set aside.

In a large bowl, whisk together egg, ricotta and spinach. Gradually stir in 2½ cups (625 mL) flour and salt with wooden spoon until a soft dough forms. Place dough on a floured surface and knead in remaining flour for 5 minutes to form a smooth dough.

Divide dough into 8 pieces; roll each into long, thin strands, about 1 inch (2.5 cm) thick. Cut into about 36 1-inch (2.5 cm) pieces.

Roll each piece across tines of a fork, gnocchi paddle or gnocchi basket. Place in a single layer on a floured baking sheet. Repeat with remaining dough. Place in the freezer for about 1 hour or until firm. Use a flat spatula or wooden spoon to gently scrape the frozen gnocchi off the baking sheet.

CONTINUED NEXT PAGE >

Spinach Ricotta Gnocchi CONTINUED

In a large pot of boiling salted water, cook gnocchi from frozen for about 8 minutes or until they float to the top and are tender throughout. Drain with a slotted spoon and toss with Homemade Tomato Sauce (see recipe p. 23) or Easy Gorgonzola Sauce (see recipe p. 124).

Make ahead: If you want to freeze the gnocchi, once they are firmly frozen, use a spatula to scrape pasta off baking sheet into a resealable plastic bag and freeze for up to 3 months.

To make plain ricotta gnocchi, like my Zia Lina sometimes does, omit spinach and use only 2 cups (500 mL) of flour to stir in to form soft dough. You may need to knead in more flour to form a smooth dough.

MAKES 2 LB (1 KG), ENOUGH FOR 4 TO 6 SERVINGS.

Sweet Potato Gnocchi with Sage Butter

Gnocchi di Patate Dolci con Salsa al Burro e Salvia

These delicate dumplings melt in your mouth and have a golden orange colour from the sweet potatoes. By using a combination of both potato and sweet potato, the dumplings end up not too sweet but just right.

2 small orange sweet potatoes, about
    1½ lb (750 kg)
3 yellow-fleshed potatoes, about
    1 lb (450 g)
1 egg yolk
2 tsp (10 mL) salt
2½ cups (625 mL) all-purpose flour
    (approx.)

Sage Butter
½ cup (125 mL) butter
¼ cup (60 mL) chopped fresh sage
¼ tsp (1 mL) pepper
½ cup (125 mL) freshly grated
    Parmesan cheese

PEEL AND CUBE sweet potatoes and potatoes. Place in a large pot and cover with water. Bring to boil and boil for about 20 minutes or until tender. Drain well and let stand for 5 minutes in a strainer.

Put potatoes through food mill or ricer, in batches into a large bowl. Let cool slightly. Stir in egg yolk and salt. Stir in enough flour to form a soft slightly sticky dough. Knead to bring dough together. Divide dough into 8 pieces. Roll into long rope about ½ inch (1 cm) thick. Cut into ½-inch (1 cm) pieces. Toss with flour. Roll along fork, gnocchi paddle or gnocchi basket to imprint. Toss with flour. Place on floured baking sheet. Repeat with remaining dough. Place in the freezer for about 1 hour or until firm.

In a large pot of boiling salted water, add gnocchi, in batches and cook for about 3 minutes or until they float. Using slotted spoon or small sieve, scoop out gnocchi and place in a large bowl. Repeat with remaining gnocchi.

Meanwhile, in large skillet melt butter over medium-high heat. Add sage and pepper; cook for 30 seconds. Pour over gnocchi and toss gently. Sprinkle with Parmesan cheese and serve.

MAKES 6 TO 8 SERVINGS.

Basil Pesto *Pesto di Basilico*

Try this basic pesto recipe and then try out the many variations you can make. It's a flavourful way to use up your basil during the summer months. By making a few batches of pesto in the summer and freezing it, you may have enough to last all year. If you do run out, basil is available year round in grocery stores.

Pesto is very versatile. It is easy to brush on meats like chicken, pork or veal while grilling or used as a sauce to serve over grilled meats or fish. Be sure to include pesto in salad dressings; just a tablespoon or two will add a huge hit of flavour.

If you are making a large batch of pesto, my late Zio Enzo, my mother's brother-in-law, taught me a great trick. He poured all the pesto into a large rectangular baking dish and froze it solid. He then popped it out of the dish like an ice cube and cut it into squares and froze it in a sealed container or bag. This way every time you need some pesto you can take out a cube big or small!

2 cups (500 mL) packed fresh basil
    leaves
¾ cup (190 mL) freshly grated
    Parmesan cheese
¼ cup (60 mL) pine nuts

2 cloves garlic, minced
¼ tsp (1 mL) salt
Pinch of pepper
¾ cup (190 mL) extra virgin olive oil
    (approx.)

IN A FOOD PROCESSOR, pulse basil leaves, cheese, pine nuts, garlic, salt and pepper. With machine running, slowly drizzle in enough of the oil until smooth. Scrape into airtight container and refrigerate for up to 3 days or freeze for up to 6 months.

MAKES 1½ CUPS (375 ML).

> Pestos are a wonderful sauce to use for hot or cold pasta dishes. For hot pasta, cook 1 lb (450 g) short or long pasta and toss with pesto. For cold pasta salads, use pesto as the dressing and add a splash of vinegar to spark up the salad's flavour.

Basil Oregano Pesto: Decrease basil to 1½ cups (375 mL) and add ½ cup (125 mL) lightly packed fresh oregano leaves.

Arugula Pesto: Omit basil. Substitute 1 cup (250 mL) packed fresh arugula leaves and 1 cup (250 mL) packed fresh Italian parsley leaves.

Spinach Pesto: Omit basil. Substitute 1 cup (250 mL) packed fresh baby spinach leaves and 1 cup (250 mL) packed fresh Italian parsley leaves.

Coriander Pesto: Omit basil and pine nuts. Substitute 2 cups (500 mL) lightly packed fresh coriander leaves.

Fresh Tomato Sauce *Salsa Fresca di Pomodoro*

With the amount of tomatoes in the garden during the heat of later summer, sauce is always on the mind of many in my family. I wash the plum tomatoes and halve them for the freezer to add later to a chili or stew. One of my favourite ways to use them is in this easy, fresh tasting tomato sauce. Adding it to fresh pasta makes for a delicious summer meal. Cooking fresh in-season tomatoes showcases a touch of sweetness but also their fresh texture and slight acidity which is a perfect marriage for a light tasting pasta sauce. This chunky sauce is perfect to pair with short pasta of any kind.

2 Tbsp (30 mL) extra virgin olive oil
1 onion, finely chopped
4 cloves garlic, minced
2 Tbsp (30 mL) chopped fresh parsley
Pinch of hot pepper flakes

2 lb (1 kg) fresh ripe plum or Roma
    tomatoes, seeded and chopped
¼ cup (60 mL) chopped fresh basil
Salt, to taste

IN A LARGE SAUCEPAN, heat oil over medium heat and cook onion, garlic, parsley and hot pepper flakes for about 5 minutes or until very soft. Stir in tomatoes and basil; bring to a simmer.

Simmer, partially covered, for 15 minutes. Season to taste with salt. Remove cover, stir and simmer for about 10 minutes or until thickened. Taste and add additional salt, if necessary.

MAKES 3 CUPS (750 ML).

Easy Gorgonzola Cheese Sauce

Salsa Facile alla Gorgonzola

This sauce is very special yet super simple. It is tasty with pastas like tagliatelle, fettuccine or even gnocchi. This rich and decadent sauce is always a favourite.

2 Tbsp (30 mL) butter
1 small shallot, diced
1½ cups (375 mL) 35% whipping cream
4 oz (125 g) Gorgonzola or other blue
   cheese, crumbled
Pinch of fresh ground pepper
2 Tbsp (30 mL) freshly grated Parmesan cheese

This is about 3/4 cup (190 mL) of Gorgonzola cheese.

IN A LARGE SKILLET, heat butter over medium heat. Cook shallot for 3 minutes or until softened. Add cream and bring to boil for about 3 minutes or until reduced slightly. Reduce heat; add Gorgonzola and pepper. Stir until melted and thickened.

Toss with your favourite cooked pasta.

MAKES 1½ CUPS (375 ML) OR ENOUGH FOR 1 LB (450 G) OF PASTA.

Noodle Soup *Zuppa di Pasta*

This homey noodle soup is simple to make for lunch or dinner. I remember bowls of hot soups that my Nonna would make for Nonno. I sat right alongside him with my big spoon eating the same soup. Sometimes it's the simplest things that taste the best. You can sprinkle the soup with more Parmesan if you desire a richer flavour.

6 cups (1.5 L) chicken or vegetable stock
   (see recipe p. 22)
4 oz (125 g) spaghetti, broken into 1-inch
   (2.5 cm) pieces
1 red bell pepper, diced
⅓ cup (80 mL) chopped Italian parsley
¼ cup (60 mL) fresh grated Parmesan cheese

It's hard to measure out spaghetti sometimes, simply divide a 1 lb (450 g) package into 4 so you will be ready to make this soup 4 times!

IN A SAUCEPAN, bring stock to a boil. Add spaghetti and cook for about 5 minutes or until pasta is tender.

Stir in pepper, parsley and cheese. Reduce heat and simmer for 5 minutes.

MAKES 4 SERVINGS.

Egg Noodle Soup Variation: Omit pepper. In a bowl, whisk 4 eggs with Parmesan cheese and parsley. Very slowly pour egg mixture into simmering stock, after spaghetti is tender. Stir constantly and cook for 2 minutes.

Bread Noodle Soup *Zuppa di Passatelli*

Homemade noodles for soup can often take some time to prepare but not these quick little noodles. By mixing together eggs, cheese and bread crumbs, you create a savory noodle that only needs a simple stock to enjoy with it. You can make the noodles in the morning and refrigerate them to cook for dinner that night but they are quick enough to make right before dinner with some helping hands.

3 eggs, lightly beaten
1 cup (250 mL) grated Parmesan cheese
Pinch of salt
Pinch of pepper
1 cup (250 mL) dry Italian-seasoned
   bread crumbs
1 Tbsp (15 mL) butter
6 cups (1.5 L) Vegetable or Chicken Stock
   (see recipe p. 22)

Look for dry Italian seasoned bread crumbs in the bakery of the grocery store. They usually are seasoned with dried herbs like oregano and basil and cheese like Romano or Parmesan. You can make your own version by using dry stale bread and whirling it in the food processor until fine crumbs are made and pulse in herbs and cheese to season.

IN LARGE BOWL, stir together eggs, cheese, salt and pepper. Add bread crumbs and butter; bring dough together with hands. Using ½ tsp (2 mL) of the dough roll into thin strands, using the palm of your hands (You may need to dampen your hands slightly to help prevent sticking). Set noodles on a plate. Repeat with remaining dough.

Meanwhile, in a large saucepan, bring stock to a simmer. Add noodles to stock and cook, stirring gently, for about 5 minutes or until *passatelli* are firm and float to the top.

MAKES 4 SERVINGS.

Belly Button Soup *Zuppa di Tortellini*

Nonna makes this soup with homemade stock. She would make it for us on cold nights and also on hot nights because it was our favourite! We have always called it "belly button" soup because of the shape of the tortellini.

If you cannot find fresh tortellini you can substitute a frozen variety.

1 lb (450 g) fresh meat or cheese tortellini

8 cups (2 L) Chicken or Vegetable Stock
  (see recipe p. 22)

2 Tbsp (30 mL) chopped parsley or basil

¼ cup (60 mL) grated Parmesan cheese

IN A LARGE POT of boiling salted water, cook tortellini for 8 minutes or until they float to the top. Using small sieve or slotted spoon, lift out tortellini to a bowl and set aside.

Meanwhile, in a large saucepan, bring chicken stock and parsley to boil. Stir in tortellini and simmer for 5 minutes.

Serve in deep soup bowls; sprinkle with Parmesan.

MAKES 4 SERVINGS.

> For a heartier soup, stir in 2 cups (500 mL) frozen mixed vegetables or chopped spinach with tortellini. Adding the frozen vegetables will increase the cooking time by about 2 minutes. If you are using frozen tortellini, increase the cooking time by about 1 minute.

Pancetta and Parmesan Pasta

Pasta con Pancetta e Parmigiano

This pasta is a great example of real down home rustic cuisine. The simple flavours produce a pasta dish to remember. Serving it with a glass of your favourite Italian red wine is a perfect match.

This sauce is a favourite of my father's because of its simple flavour and how quickly the meal comes together. His pasta of choice to match up with it? Bucatini, a long thin tube of pasta. I think he likes it because it's messy when you slurp it up.

1 Tbsp (15 mL) **extra virgin olive oil**

4 oz (125 g) **pancetta, diced**

1 onion, **fined chopped**

4 cloves garlic, **minced**

¼ tsp (1 mL) **hot pepper flakes**

1 can (28 oz / 796 mL) tomatoes, chopped

12 oz (375 g) **spaghetti**

Grated Parmigiano Reggiano, to taste

Chopped fresh Italian parsley, to taste

You will need 3 cups (750 mL) canned tomatoes for this recipe. Chop the tomatoes and be sure to add both the tomatoes and juice to the sauce. Look for chopped or diced canned tomatoes for a quicker sauce. This will give you more chunks and less juice.

Try other pastas such as linguine, bucatini, penne or tagliatelle instead of spaghetti.

IN A LARGE SKILLET OR SAUCEPAN, heat oil over medium heat. Add pancetta; cook for 5 minutes or until crisp. Add onion and garlic; cook for 5 minutes or until softened. Add hot pepper flakes; stir to coat. Stir in tomatoes and cook for about 15 minutes or until thickened.

Meanwhile, in large pot of boiling salted water, cook pasta for about 8 minutes or until *al dente*. Drain well and return to pot. Add sauce and stir to coat well. Stir in cheese and parsley, if desired.

MAKES 4 SERVINGS.

Spaghetti Carbonara *Spaghetti alla Carbonara*

This is a restaurant quality dish that you can serve at home. This is easy; it only has 6 ingredients. You can find pancetta in the deli section of the grocery store or packaged and already sliced for ease of use.

12 oz (375 g) spaghetti
6 slices pancetta
4 eggs
⅓ cup (80 mL) grated Parmesan or
   Romano cheese

¼ cup (60 mL) chopped fresh Italian
   parsley
Pinch of pepper

IN A LARGE POT of boiling salted water, cook spaghetti for about 8 minutes or until *al dente*. Drain and return to pot over medium heat.

Meanwhile, in skillet, cook pancetta for about 5 minutes or until slightly crisp. Drain on paper towel-lined plate; chop and set aside.

In a bowl, whisk together eggs, cheese, parsley and pepper; add to hot, drained pasta and toss for about 30 seconds until pasta is coated. Add pancetta and toss to combine.

MAKES 4 SERVINGS.

Green Risotto *Risotto Verde*

Use your favourite green vegetable or leafy greens like rapini, kale or swiss chard in place of the asparagus. This risotto should be slightly soupy; that's how I enjoyed it growing up.

2 Tbsp (25 mL) extra virgin olive oil

1 onion, finely chopped

2 cloves garlic, minced

1½ cups (375 mL) Arborio or Italian-style rice

6 cups (1.5 L) Chicken or Vegetable Stock, hot (see recipe p. 22)

You can keep the stock on low heat in a pot beside your risotto to ladle in as you are stirring.

1 cup (250 mL) finely chopped asparagus

1 cup (250 mL) finely shredded spinach

½ cup (125 mL) fresh grated Parmesan cheese

¼ cup (60 mL) chopped fresh basil or mint

IN A LARGE SAUCEPAN, heat oil over medium heat. Add onion and garlic and cook stirring for about 5 minutes or until softened. Add rice; stir to coat for about 1 minute. Using a ladle, pour in about 1 cup (250 mL) of the stock. Increase heat of rice to just above medium, but not quite medium-high and cook, stirring, until most of liquid is evaporated.

Cook, stirring for about 15 minutes, using as much of the stock as necessary to create a creamy texture, adding about ½ cup (125 mL) at a time. Stir in asparagus and spinach and cook for about 5 minutes, adding more stock to moisten, if necessary. Cook rice until tender but firm and remove from heat. Stir in cheese until melted and smooth. Sprinkle with basil or mint.

MAKES 4 TO 6 SERVINGS.

After I watched *Big Night,* a movie about two Italian brothers trying to make their Italian restaurant a success in America, I was inspired to make three coloured risottos that the brothers included in their famous dinner scene. Celebrate the colours of the Italian flag: make Risotto Bianco ("white") and Rosso ("red") by reducing the stock for each recipe by about 1 cup (250 mL). Present on a large platter together.

For Risotto Bianco omit asparagus, spinach and basil. For Risotto Rosso make Risotto Bianco and add ½ cup (125 mL) pasta sauce, ¼ cup (60 mL) tomato paste and 1 cup (250 mL) chopped tomatoes.

HEARTIER PASTA DISHES AND CASSEROLES

I have to get dinner on the table each night and it can be busy. My Nonna was able to stay at home and cook for her whole family, as did some of my zias while I was growing up. I also had female family members that worked and had to come home and get dinner on the table, too. I was an onlooker for awhile but eventually I caught the cooking bug. While cooking with my family, I started realizing that these dinners were going to be the staple of much of my life. I don't think much has changed from when Nonna was cooking dinner other than the time it takes to cook the meals.

Letting a sauce simmer all day or creating a meal with many dishes might not be in the cards for everyone today. My mother worked but was still able to create memorable meals with the same flavours that were a bit faster for our busier lifestyle. Using slightly different cooking methods and techniques, many of those traditional Southern Italian flavours have survived in dishes that may not take as long to cook.

This chapter is a small collection of some of our favourite weeknight meals at our house; a reflection of what I enjoyed eating as a child and what my children also enjoy today. The flavours are what make the memories strong but, more importantly, who you are eating those meals with will cement the strength of your food and family.

PER LA FAMIGLIA

Norma's Rigatoni *Rigatoni alla Norma*

This classic Italian dish, named after the opera "Norma," uses a favourite southern Italian ingredient. When I first made this, I thought this was going to be a simple dish without much flavour, but I was happily surprised. Between the texture of the eggplant and the salty bite of ricotta salata, this pasta became a new favourite of mine.

1 small eggplant, about 8 oz (250 g)

¾ tsp (4 mL) salt, divided

⅓ cup (80 mL) all purpose flour (approx.), for dusting

¼ cup (60 mL) extra virgin olive oil

1 onion, finely chopped

1 can (28 oz / 796 mL) tomatoes, crushed

¼ tsp (1 mL) pepper

1 lb (450 g) rigatoni pasta

1 cup (250 mL) grated ricotta salata

½ cup (125 mL) chopped fresh basil

Use 3 cups (750 mL) of canned tomatoes and then crush them for a chunky texture to the sauce. Crushed tomatoes are more of a puree and will not give you the same texture and flavour.

You will need 5 cups (1.25 L) rigatoni pasta for this recipe.

Look for ricotta salata in Italian delis or larger grocery stores. It is a drier, firm salted version of ricotta cheese. You can use Asiago or Romano in place of the ricotta salata. You will need a small chunk, approximately 3.5 oz (100 g) for this recipe.

PEEL EGGPLANT and finely julienne peel. Finely dice remaining eggplant flesh. Sprinkle flesh with ½ tsp (2 mL) salt to soften. Set aside for about 15 minutes. Rinse off and lightly pat dry. Sprinkle with flour to coat and shake off any excess.

In a large non-stick skillet, heat oil over medium-high heat and brown diced eggplant and skin in batches until crispy. Remove with a slotted spoon to paper towel-lined plate. Reserve crisp eggplant skin for garnish.

Return skillet with remaining oil to medium heat and cook onion, diced eggplant, tomato, remaining salt and pepper and cook, stirring often for about 15 minutes.

Meawhile, in a large pot of boiling salted water cook pasta for about 10 minutes or until *al dente* (tender but firm). Drain well and stir into eggplant sauce to coat well.

Spoon onto a large platter and grate ricotta salata over top. Sprinkle with basil. Top with crisp eggplant skin to garnish.

MAKES 4 TO 6 SERVINGS.

Spinach Ricotta Cannelloni *Cannelloni di Ricotta e Spinaci*

My mom showed me how to make this and we decided that it would be easy to substitute store-bought fresh lasagne sheets in a pinch. These cannelloni are a family favourite for any night of the week. They freeze well and make an easy Sunday dinner. Make sure there's bread on the table to sop up any leftover sauce!

1 batch Pasta Dough (see recipe p. 110)

Filling
½ cup (125 mL) grated Parmesan cheese
¼ cup (60 mL) chopped Italian parsley
2 eggs, lightly beaten
1 tub (11 oz / 330 g) baby spinach cooked, drained and chopped

You can use 16 cups (4 L) of lightly packed spinach for the tub.

1 tub (475 g) ricotta cheese
1 cup (250 mL) shredded mozzarella cheese
Pinch of salt

You will need 1½ cups (375 mL) of ricotta cheese.

Pinch of pepper
4 cups (1 L) Homemade Tomato Sauce (see recipe p. 23) or bottled pasta sauce

CUT DOUGH INTO 4 equal pieces. Using pasta machine, roll 1 piece at a time through first setting twice. Continue through settings until smooth, thin pasta piece is formed. Lay flat on floured surface; let dry for about 15–30 minutes. Continue with remaining dough.

Cut each strip of dough into 6-inch (15 cm) rectangles to make a total of 16 cannelloni.

In large pot of boiling salted water, cook pasta sheets in batches, for about 2 minutes. Lift out of the water and lay flat on a damp tea towel.

Filling: Meanwhile, reserve 2 Tbsp (30 mL) each of the Parmesan and parsley and set aside.

In large bowl, stir together eggs, spinach, ricotta, mozzarella, remaining Parmesan and parsley, salt and pepper. Place about 3 Tbsp (45 mL) in centre of each pasta piece. Roll up to form a cylinder.

Preheat oven to 350°F (180°C).

Pour 1 cup (250 mL) of the pasta sauce in the bottom of a 13 × 9-inch (3 L) baking dish to cover bottom. Place cannelloni snugly in the pan. Pour remaining sauce over top. Sprinkle with reserved Parmesan cheese and parsley. Cover and bake for about 45 minutes or until bubbly and hot.

MAKES 8 SERVINGS.

Pumpkin Cannelloni with Chunky Sage Tomato Cream Sauce *Cannelloni di Zucca con Salsa Rose*

I don't remember growing winter squash or pumpkins until I had my own family, but we did use them in different dishes. We would sauté squash with garlic and anchovies to be tossed with pasta; the combination was perfect. In this recipe, a rich squash filling makes these cannelloni mouth-watering and a perfect vegetarian offering during the holidays or for a Sunday lunch. Egg roll wrappers make a fast pasta substitute with no precooking required.

Chunky Sage Tomato Cream Sauce

3 Tbsp (45 mL) butter

1 Tbsp (15 mL) chopped fresh sage leaves
or 2 tsp (10 mL) dried sage leaves

1 can (19 oz / 540 mL) stewed tomatoes

½ cup (125 mL) 35% whipping cream

If you buy a larger can of stewed tomatoes you will only need 2 cups (500 mL) for this recipe. If you want richer tomato sauce you can add the remaining tomatoes from the can.

Cannelloni

2 Tbsp (30 mL) butter

1 onion, finely chopped

3 cloves garlic, minced

2 Tbsp (30 mL) chopped fresh Italian parsley

2 cups (500 mL) diced fresh cut and peeled
pumpkin or squash

½ cup (125 mL) Vegetable Stock (see recipe
p. 22)

1 cup (250 mL) diced cream cheese

⅓ cup (80 mL) fresh grated Parmesan cheese

½ cup (125 mL) seasoned dry bread crumbs

¼ tsp (1 mL) salt

¼ tsp (1 mL) pepper

12 egg roll wrappers

Use the remaining wrappers in the package to make other types of pasta. They can be used for ravioli or cut it into strips for a fresh pasta dish another weeknight.

Chunky Sage Tomato Cream Sauce: In a saucepan, melt butter over medium heat and cook sage for 2 minutes until fragrant and golden. Add tomatoes and mash with potato masher. Add cream and bring to the boil. Remove from heat and set aside.

Cannelloni: In a large non-stick skillet, melt butter over medium heat and cook onion, garlic and parsley for 3 minutes or until softened. Add pumpkin and stock and bring to a simmer. Cover and cook for about 5 minutes or until pumpkin is tender and almost all of the stock has evaporated. Remove from heat and stir in both cheeses. Add bread crumbs, salt and pepper and stir until well combined.

Preheat oven to 350°F (180°C). Grease a baking dish; set aside.

Spoon 3 Tbsp (45 mL) of the filling along 1 side of egg roll wrappers and roll up. Place in prepared baking dish. Repeat with remaining filling and wrappers, nestling each other close together. Pour Sage-Tomato Cream Sauce over top of the cannelloni and cover with foil. Bake for about 30 minutes or until pasta is tender and sauce is bubbling.

MAKES 6 SERVINGS (12 CANNELLONI).

Vegetable Pasta *Pasta con Verdure*

This rustic and delicious pasta dish is great for dinner. The kick of heat from the hot pepper flakes can be reduced if your family doesn't enjoy spice. Try other greens like rapini or the tamer spinach for a change in flavour.

2 small bunches fresh greens, such as
   Swiss chard, dandelion or kale
1 pkg (350 g) fresh fettuccine pasta or
   1 batch Pasta Dough (see recipe p. 110)
⅓ cup (80 mL) extra virgin olive oil

4 cloves garlic, minced
2 tsp (10 mL) anchovy paste
½ tsp (2 mL) hot pepper flakes
2 Tbsp (30 mL) grated Parmesan cheese

TRIM TOUGH STEMS from greens. Wash well and chop to make 12 cups (3 L) of lightly packed greens.

In a large pot of boiling water, cook greens for about 8 minutes or until tender. Using a slotted spoon, remove greens to colander and set aside. Bring water back to boil and salt the water. Cook fettuccine for about 5 minutes or until *al dente* (tender but firm). Reserving some of the cooking water, drain and set both aside.

Meanwhile, in a large non-stick skillet, heat oil over medium heat. Cook garlic, anchovy paste and hot pepper flakes for about 2 minutes, stirring to combine anchovy paste into oil. Add greens and cook, stirring for about 5 minutes or until very tender. Add fettuccine and toss well to coat. Add some of the reserved cooking water to moisten if necessary.

Sprinkle with cheese before serving.

MAKES 4 SERVINGS.

Nonna's Meat Sauce with Polenta

Sugo Della Nonna con Carne e Polenta

The trick to my Nonna's sauce is that she uses ingredients she loves and makes enough to feed a crowd. This is a hearty stick-to-your-ribs dish that brings back childhood memories every time I make it. Letting the pork riblets cook in the sauce helps produce a robust flavour.

2 Tbsp (30 mL) extra virgin olive oil

2½ lb (1.25 kg) pork riblets or veal bones
   (with some meat still on)

1 onion, chopped

2 cloves garlic, minced

1 Tbsp (15 mL) dried oregano

½ tsp (2 mL) hot pepper flakes

½ cup (125 mL) dry white wine

2 cans (28 oz / 796 mL each) plum
   tomatoes, pureed

4 sprigs fresh parsley

1 sprig fresh basil

1 tsp (5 mL) salt

Polenta

8 cups (2 L) water

1½ cups (375 mL) cornmeal

1 tsp (5 mL) salt

½ cup (125 mL) freshly grated Parmesan
   cheese

2 Tbsp (30 mL) chopped fresh basil

You will need 6 cups (1.5 L) of canned tomatoes for this recipe. To puree them I like to put them in the blender in batches until they are smooth. I don't use crushed tomatoes for this recipe as it is too thick for the long slow simmer this sauce does.

IN A LARGE SHALLOW SAUCEPAN, heat oil over medium-high heat and brown riblets well; remove to a plate. Return saucepan to medium heat and cook onion, garlic, oregano and hot pepper flakes for about 5 minutes or until softened. Add wine and cook, stirring to scrape up any brown bits. Add tomatoes, parsley, basil and salt; stir to combine. Return riblets to saucepan, and bring to a boil. Reduce heat, cover and simmer for about 4 hours or until meat is falling off the bone.

Polenta: In a deep pot, bring water to a boil; whisk in cornmeal and salt. Using a wooden spoon, cook, stirring for about 15 minutes or until thickened and polenta mounds on a spoon. Stir in cheese and basil.

Remove bones from sauce and break up meat into smaller pieces, if desired. Spoon sauce over polenta to serve.

MAKES 8 TO 10 SERVINGS.

Super-Fast Sausage and Ricotta Lasagne

Lasagne Rapida con Salsiccia e Ricotta

Make dinner in a flash with this great idea. Zia Emily, my mother's youngest sister, had told me about her easy lasagne and how she got my Nonna to eat it and thought it was fresh pasta noodles. What was her secret? Wonton wrappers! No need to boil water; just take them out of the package and make a lasagne for dinner.

1½ cups (375 mL) chunky vegetable
　pasta sauce
⅓ cup (80 mL) water
¼ tsp (1 mL) hot pepper flakes or fresh
　ground pepper
1 pkg (8 oz / 250 g) wonton wrappers
1 tub (475 g) ricotta or cottage cheese
1 cup (250 mL) finely chopped cooked
　Italian sausage
2 cups (500 mL) shredded Italian
　cheese blend

You will need 1½ cups (375 mL) ricotta or cottage cheese for this recipe.

You can substitute cooked ground beef for the sausage.

To make your own Italian cheese blend, combine shredded mozzarella, provolone and Parmesan cheeses. In some premade blends they include a slightly stronger flavoured cheese like swiss, but gouda or fontina also work.

PREHEAT OVEN TO 350°F (180°C).

In a bowl, combine pasta sauce with water and hot pepper flakes. Spread about ½ cup (125 mL) sauce in an 8-inch (2 L) baking dish. Cover bottom with wonton wrappers, overlapping slightly; then another ⅓ cup (80 mL) sauce. Top with one-third of the ricotta and chopped sausage. Sprinkle with ½ cup (125 mL) cheese. Repeat layers twice.

Arrange remaining wonton wrappers over top; spread with remaining sauce and cheese. Bake for about 30 minutes or until bubbly. Let stand 5 minutes before cutting.

MAKES 4 SERVINGS.

Vegetarian Variation: Omit sausage. Use 6 hard-boiled eggs, sliced.

Slow Cooker Lasagne

Lasagne Nella Pentola a Cottura Lenta

Lasagne couldn't get easier than putting it in the slow cooker; perfect when you come home from work to enjoy a hot meal with your family. Try adding other greens or cooked vegetables for a twist of flavours.

8 oz (225 g) ground veal or beef
1 onion, finely chopped
3 cloves garlic, minced
2 tsp (10 mL) dried oregano
¼ tsp (1 mL) hot pepper flakes
1 jar (700 mL) tomato passata
1 cup (250 mL) water or chicken broth
1 tub (500 g) 1% cottage cheese or
  ricotta cheese
1 pkg (5 oz / 142 g) baby spinach, chopped
¼ cup (60 mL) chopped fresh basil or parsley
2 Tbsp (30 mL) grated Parmesan cheese
10 lasagna noodles
½ cup (125 mL) shredded part skim mozzarella

You can use 2 3/4 cups (675 mL) of tomato puree or strained tomatoes for the jar of passata.

You will need 2 cups (500 mL) of cottage or ricotta cheese.

You will need 8 cups (2 L) of baby spinach

LIGHTLY SPRAY INSIDE OF SLOW COOKER with cooking spray.

In a large non-stick skillet, brown veal breaking it up with a spoon over medium heat. Add onion, garlic, oregano and hot pepper flakes for 5 minutes or until softened. Add passata and water; remove from heat.

In a bowl, stir together cottage cheese, spinach, basil and Parmesan cheese.

Spread some of the meat sauce over bottom of slow cooker. Lay lasagna noodles in a single layer, breaking as necessary to fit. Top with one-quarter of the sauce and one-third of the cheese mixture. Repeat layers twice, ending with meat sauce on top. Cover and cook on low for 6–8 hours or on high for 3–4 hours. About 15 minutes before serving lasagne, sprinkle mozzarella over top, cover and let cook on low until melted.

MAKES 8 TO 10 SERVINGS.

Meat Lasagne *Lasagne con Carne*

This straight-forward lasagne recipe uses only one meat and homemade pasta noodles. If you want to use fresh store-bought pasta sheets, they do vary in sizes. Use a baking dish that will accommodate the size of the pasta or trim them to fit. You can always keep any extra pasta and cut it up in small pieces to make "pasta maltagliata" (badly cut pasta, a real dish in Italy). It doesn't matter what the pasta looks like, it will still taste good.

2 Tbsp (30 mL) extra virgin olive oil

1 onion, finely chopped

2 cloves garlic, minced

2 tsp (10 mL) dried oregano

1 lb (450 g) extra lean ground beef ———— *You can substitute turkey or veal for the beef.*

Pinch of salt

Pinch of pepper

6 cups (1.5 L) of Homemade Tomato Sauce ———— *6 cups of pasta sauce is 1 1/2 batches of the recipe on p. 23.*
   (see recipe p. 23)

1 pkg (350 g) fresh pasta lasagne sheets or
   1 batch Pasta Dough (see recipe p. 110)

1 ball (340 g) mozzarella, shredded ———— *One ball of mozzarella shredded will usually make about 3 cups (750 mL).*

Half a (475 g) container of ricotta cheese or ————
   1 batch Fresh Creamy Ricotta Cheese (see *You will need 3/4 cup (190 mL) of ricotta cheese.*
   recipe p. 29)

2 Tbsp (30 mL) grated Parmesan cheese

IN A LARGE NON-STICK SKILLET, heat oil over medium-high heat and cook onion, garlic and oregano for 2 minutes. Add beef and cook, stirring for about 8 minutes or until browned. Add salt and pepper. Pour in pasta sauce and bring to a gentle simmer. Simmer for 5 minutes; remove from heat.

Preheat oven to 350°F (180°C).

Pour 1 cup (250 mL) of the sauce in the bottom of a baking dish. Top with pasta sheets, another cup (250 mL) of sauce, some of the ricotta cheese and mozzarella cheese. Repeat with another 4 pasta sheets, sauce and cheeses. Sprinkle remaining ricotta cheese on top and last pasta sheet. Spread with another 1 cup (250 mL) sauce and remaining mozzarella cheese. Cover with foil and place on baking sheet.

Bake for 45 minutes. Uncover and bake for another 30 minutes or until golden brown and knife inserted in centre is hot. Refrigerate for up to 1 day before baking.

MAKES 8 SERVINGS.

Three Meat Lasagne *Lasagne con Tre Tipi di Carne*

Using my Nonna's rich tasting three-meat sauce makes this family-size lasagne a large-gathering favourite. I've made it quicker by using wonton wrappers for the pasta layers. You can use the sauce over your favourite pasta for dinner if you're pressed for time. Or double up on the sauce and freeze half for another lasagne later in the month.

¼ cup (60 mL) extra virgin olive oil

8 oz (225 g) ground pork

8 oz (225 g) ground veal

8 oz (225 g) lean ground beef

You can substitute other ground meats like turkey or chicken for any of these, or make the sauce with just two of the three meats.

1 onion, chopped

3 large cloves garlic, minced

1 Tbsp (15 mL) dried oregano leaves

1 tsp (5 mL) salt

½ tsp (2 mL) hot pepper flakes

⅓ cup (80 mL) dry white wine

2 jars (700 mL each) tomato passata

Passata is available in grocery stores near other pasta sauces and is simply a tomato puree with no seeds or skin. If you can't find it, puree 2 cans (28 oz / 796 mL each) of plum tomatoes as a substitute.

½ cup (125 mL) water

6 sprigs fresh Italian parsley

2 sprigs fresh basil

1 pkg (1 lb / 450 g) wonton wrappers

1 tub (475 g) ricotta cheese

2½ cups (625 mL) shredded mozzarella cheese

¼ cup (60 mL) freshly grated Parmesan cheese

You will need 1½ cups (375 mL) of ricotta for this recipe.

IN A POT, HEAT 2 TBSP (30 mL) oil over medium-high heat and cook pork, veal, beef, onion, garlic, oregano, salt and hot pepper flakes, breaking up with a spoon. Cook for about 8 minutes or until ground meats are no longer pink. Add wine and cook, stirring, for 1 minute. Add tomato passata.

Pour water into one of the passata jars and seal. Shake and pour into other passata jar and repeat. Pour all the liquid into the pot. Add parsley, basil and remaining oil and stir to combine. Bring to a boil. Reduce heat, cover partially, and simmer for 45 minutes. Remove from heat. Remove herbs.

Preheat oven to 350°F (180°C).

Ladle some of the sauce on bottom of 13 × 9-inch (33 × 23 cm) baking dish. Layer wonton wrappers in a single layer on top. Ladle more sauce over top to coat. Dollop one-third of the ricotta over top. Sprinkle with one-quarter of the mozzarella and Parmesan cheeses. Repeat layers twice and top with wonton wrappers and remaining sauce. Sprinkle remaining mozzarella and Parmesan cheeses over top.

Bake for about 35 minutes or until bubbly and golden on top. Remove from oven and let stand for 10 minutes before cutting and serving.

MAKES 8 TO 10 SERVINGS.

Baked Pasta with Sausage and Ricotta

Pasta al Forno con Salsiccia e Ricotta

Larger pasta dishes in casseroles are perfect to serve at large gatherings. There are so many variations; you can change up the flavour and pasta combination each time.

1 Tbsp (15 mL) extra virgin olive oil

1 lb (450 g) Italian sausage meat

1 onion, chopped

3 Tbsp (45 mL) chopped fresh parsley

3 cloves garlic, minced

¼ tsp (1 mL) hot pepper flakes

½ cup (125 mL) dry white wine

1 jar (700 mL) tomato passata

3 fresh basil leaves

¼ tsp (1 mL) salt

1 pkg (450 g) penne pasta

1 tub (475 g) ricotta cheese

½ cup (125 mL) fresh grated Parmesan cheese

2 hard cooked eggs, peeled and chopped

1 cup (250 mL) shredded mozzarella or
   provolone cheese

If bulk sausage meat isn't available, use fresh Italian sausages and remove the casings.

You will need 2 3/4 cups (675 mL) of tomato puree for this recipe if a jar of passata is unavailable.

You can substitute 4 1/2 cups (1.125 L) of penne pasta for a package.

You will need 1 1/2 cups (375 mL) of ricotta cheese if the package is unavailable.

IN A LARGE SHALLOW SKILLET OR SAUCEPAN, heat oil over medium-high heat and cook sausage with onion, parsley, garlic and hot pepper flakes, breaking up sausage with spoon, for about 8 minutes or until browned. Add wine and simmer until absorbed. Stir in passata, basil and salt and simmer, stirring occasionally, for 15 minutes.

Preheat oven to 400°F (200°C).

Meanwhile, in a large pot of boiling salted water, cook pasta for about 8 minutes or until *al dente*. Drain and return to pot. Add sausage sauce, ricotta, parmesan and eggs; stirring to combine. Spread into a 13 × 9-inch (33 × 23 cm) casserole dish and sprinkle with mozzarella. Cover with foil and bake for 15 minutes. Uncover and bake for another 10 minutes or until cheese is melted.

MAKES 8 TO 10 SERVINGS.

Make ahead: If making this ahead of time, cover and refrigerate for up to 1 day. Bake in 350°F (180°C) oven for about 40 minutes or until heated through. Uncover and bake for another 10 minutes to add some colour and crisp up the top, if desired.

MAIN COURSES

I don't remember my own baptism but I sort of remember my sister's. We went to a hall and had a wonderful meal. I'm sure she was all dressed up, of course, but I only remember the family and food and how much I loved the party.

When I had my children, I knew that I wanted to have celebratory baptisms but perhaps not on a grand scale. For both of my son's baptisms, porchetta (Italian roast pork) was on the menu. When my daughter, Adriana, was born, I was a bit tired so we went to a local hall and enjoyed roast pork, again. Do you see the theme? Yes, it suits my family well.

That is the great part about these events; the church celebration is in the afternoon so it's the perfect time for either a late lunch or an early dinner. I love having these gatherings after the church ceremony at home. Everyone seems relaxed and family is always ready to pitch in. Whether it's getting out the antipasti or cleaning up the dishes, everyone helps out.

So far in my small family, we've had three baptisms, two first communions and we are waiting for our third. I look forward to the future and their confirmations. With the food being a major part of these celebrations, the main courses are in the starring role, much like the children who are celebrating. By following the faith and tradition of our family into adulthood, they will not only enjoy the family around them but the food that continues to appear at our celebrations.

Depending on whether you are enjoying a weeknight family meal or a celebratory get-together, the main courses can vary tremendously. For a casual affair you might serve just one main course with a pasta or vegetable. In my family, we most often create a table full of options in order to make everyone happy. I recommend that you do what is realistic for you but always have fun doing it.

Rapini Frittata *Frittata di Rapini*

Rapini is a slightly bitter green that is used often as an Italian side dish, or in other pasta or egg dishes. It is also known as broccoli rabe because the florets in the bunch are reminiscent of broccoli. I love rapini cooked any way because of its slightly bitter and mustardy flavour. Substitute other veggies like spinach, kale, broccoli or Swiss chard for the rapini if you want to experiment with this recipe.

This versatile frittata is spectacular cut and placed on a crusty bun for a dinner sandwich, maybe with a little pasta sauce on top. Enjoy it hot or cold with a side salad or serve it up in little squares as an appetizer.

1 bunch rapini, trimmed
2 Tbsp (25 mL) extra virgin olive oil
2 cloves garlic, minced
¼ tsp (1 mL) hot pepper flakes
6 eggs
¼ cup (60 mL) grated Parmesan cheese
¼ tsp (1 mL) salt
Pinch of fresh ground pepper

Trim about 1 inch (2.5 cm) off the bottom stalks of the rapini before cooking to remove dry split stems.

IN A POT OF BOILING WATER, cook rapini until stalks are tender but firm, about 6 minutes. Drain well, gently pushing down on rapini to remove even more water. Chop rapini coarsely.

In non-stick skillet, heat oil over medium heat and cook garlic and pepper flakes until fragrant, about 1 minute. Add rapini and toss to coat, stirring until rapini is beginning to brown and get crispy, about 8 minutes.

Meanwhile in a bowl, whisk together eggs, cheese, salt and pepper. Pour into the skillet with rapini. Cook, lifting edge with rubber spatula letting any runny egg drip to the bottom, until bottom is light golden and top is set. Place a large plate overtop of skillet and flip skillet to drop frittata onto plate. Slide frittata back into skillet and cook until golden, about 3 minutes.

MAKES 4 SERVINGS.

Bean Puttanesca *Puttasnesca di Fagioli*

Many of my family members are vegetarians so I like to add Italian flavour and ease to dishes for them as well. The traditional flavour of puttanesca sauce, a classic, intensely flavoured Italian sauce that is served with pasta, makes this dish a quick weeknight meal. The rich flavour of capers, olives and hot peppers sparks up the beans and creates a hearty vegetarian meal.

2 Tbsp (30 mL) extra virgin olive oil

1 small onion, diced

3 cloves garlic, minced

½ jalapeño or other hot pepper, seeded
   and diced

1 can (28 oz / 796 mL) diced tomatoes

1 small can (14 oz / 400 mL) black-eyed peas,
   drained and rinsed

¼ cup (60 mL) chopped and pitted oil-cured
   olives

2 Tbsp (30 mL) chopped fresh oregano

2 Tbsp (30 mL) chopped fresh Italian parsley

1 Tbsp (15 mL) capers

Pinch of salt

3 cups (750 mL) cooked couscous (see below)

¼ cup (60 mL) freshly grated Parmigiano
   Reggiano cheese

You can substitute 3 cups (750 mL) chopped fresh tomatoes for the can of diced tomatoes.

You can use 1 1/2 cups (375 mL) cooked black-eyed peas for the can.

IN A LARGE SHALLOW SAUCEPAN, heat oil over medium heat and cook onion, garlic and jalapeño pepper for 5 minutes or until softened. Add tomatoes, black-eyed peas, olives, oregano, parsley, capers and salt and bring to boil. Reduce heat and simmer for 10 minutes or until slightly thickened. Spoon overtop couscous and sprinkle with cheese before serving.

MAKES 4 SERVINGS.

How to make couscous: In a saucepan, bring 1 cup (250 mL) vegetable stock or water to boil. Add 1 cup (250 mL) couscous and remove from heat; cover and let stand for 10 minutes. Fluff with fork before serving. Add salt and pepper to taste.

Chicken Under Bricks *Pollo al Mattone*

I love making this outside on my grill and it becomes quite the topic of discussion. Some-day it will be great to have a brick oven in my backyard, but for now the grill or stovetop works well for this recipe. Traditionally, "Chicken Under Bricks" was cooked in a brick oven and flattened with more bricks. Flattening the chicken not only helps decrease cook-ing time, it creates a wonderful crust that adds flavour and texture to the chicken.

You can also do this with two cornish hens instead of the chicken for a dinner twist and reduce the cooking time by about 10 minutes.

One 3 lb (1.5 kg) whole chicken	2 Tbsp (30 mL) chopped fresh rosemary
2 Tbsp (30 mL) extra virgin olive oil, divided	½ tsp (2 mL) salt
	½ tsp (2 mL) pepper
2 Tbsp (30 mL) chopped fresh sage	1 foil wrapped brick

USING KITCHEN SHEARS OR STRONG SCISSORS, cut the chicken along each side of the backbone; remove backbone. Turn chicken over; push on breastbone to open chicken out flat. Tuck wings behind back of chicken or trim the wing tips. Place chicken in large shal-low baking dish.

Brush chicken all over with half of the oil. Rub chicken evenly with sage, rosemary, salt and pepper.

For extra flavour rub zest of lemon under the skin with the herbs.

In a large skillet, heat remaining oil over medium heat. Place chicken, skin-side down, in pan. Place brick on top of chicken. Cook for 20 minutes.

You can do this on the grill instead of the stove. Use medium heat and make sure your grill is preheated and oiled well before starting.

Remove brick; turn chicken over. Replace brick on chicken; cook for about 25 minutes longer or until no longer pink inside.

You may want to use two pairs of tongs to turn chicken over more easily.

MAKES 4 TO 6 SERVINGS.

Prosciutto and Ricotta Chicken Roll Ups

Involtini di Pollo con Prosciutto e Ricotta

I love using Italian ingredients like ricotta, basil, prosciutto, garlic and Parmesan cheese to make dinner. These can easily become staples in your kitchen to make dinner fast and easy. Marinate the chicken breasts in the morning so all you have to do is stuff them when you get home from work. You can quickly fill the chicken breasts and have them ready to put in the oven for a quick dinner with Italian flare.

4 boneless skinless chicken breasts

¼ cup (60 mL) your favourite Italian-style salad dressing

½ cup (125 mL) ricotta cheese

2 Tbsp (30 mL) chopped fresh basil

2 Tbsp (30 mL) chopped Italian parsley

2 Tbsp (30 mL) fresh grated Parmesan cheese

¼ tsp (1 mL) pepper

4 slices prosciutto

¼ cup (60 mL) extra virgin olive oil

1 tub (11 oz / 330 g) baby spinach

1 cup (250 mL) grape tomatoes, halved

4 cloves garlic, minced

½ tsp (2 mL) salt

You can make your own Italian salad dressing for this recipe by mixing together 2 Tbsp (30 mL) oil and 2 Tbsp (30 mL) red or white wine vinegar with a pinch of oregano, salt and pepper.

You can use 12 cups (3 L) of baby spinach for this recipe instead of the tub.

USING A MEAT MALLET, pound chicken breasts to ¼ inch (6 mm) thick. Place in a shallow dish and add salad dressing, turning to coat chicken. Let stand for 10 minutes.

Meanwhile, in a bowl, stir together ricotta cheese, basil, parsley and Parmesan.

Remove chicken from sauce and let excess drip off. Sprinkle with pepper. Lay chicken breasts flat on the work surface and top each with a slice of prosciutto. Divide ricotta mixture among chicken breasts along centre of each crosswise. Roll up chicken breasts and secure with a toothpick.

Preheat oven to 400°F (200°C). In an ovenproof skillet, heat half of the oil over medium-high heat. Brown chicken rolls on all sides and place skillet in oven for about 10 minutes or until chicken is no longer pink inside.

Meanwhile, in a large non-stick skillet heat remaining oil over medium-high heat and add spinach, tomatoes, garlic and salt and toss quickly for about 2 minutes or until slightly wilted and warmed. Divide among 4 plates and top each with a chicken roll.

MAKES 4 SERVINGS.

Fresh Pork Sausages *Salsiccia Fresche di Maiale*

Starting in late December or early January you'll see mounds of fresh pork cuts available in grocery stores (and my house) which means it is high time for some fresh sausage making. In our family, most weekends in January are filled with trimming, grinding and stuffing pork into casings for fresh and dried sausages and various salami. There is now an annual event with my dad's cousins, the Spinas, when they will get together and my dad helps them make massive quantities of delicious sausages. That's how we kick off the salami season (as I call it). I am happy my oldest son Matthew has shown interest and it looks like my second son Nicolas will soon follow by giving a hand to their Nonno.

Even my husband has gotten involved by helping grind the meat. The meat grinder is an important piece of equipment to make the sausages. Sometimes they can be found as an attachment to your stand mixer. When searching for your own, check out cookware shops, Italian delis and specialty stores for the best selection.

1 orange

13–16 feet (4–5 m) small intestines
   (sausage casings)

One 8 lb (4 kg) boneless pork loin rib end
   roast or pork shoulder blade roast

2 Tbsp (30 mL) salt

2½ tsp (12 mL) hot pepper flakes

2 tsp (10 mL) paprika

2 tsp (10 mL) fennel seeds

⅓ cup (80 mL) dry red wine

2 Tbsp (30 mL) store-bought hot
   pepper sauce

REMOVE ORANGE ZEST FROM ORANGE and place zest in bowl of warm water. Squeeze juice from orange into water. Rinse intestines (sausage casings) with warm water to remove salt and add intestines to water mixture.

Cut pork into small chunks and feed through a meat grinder. Put about one-third of the ground meat through the grinder again for a nice texture to the sausages. (You can ask the butcher to do this step for you).

Place the ground pork in a very large bowl or basin. Add salt, hot pepper flakes, paprika and fennel seeds and start to mix the spices in with your hands. Add wine and hot pepper sauce and mix well until mixture is evenly distributed. Take a handful of the pork mixture and cook it in a small skillet until it is golden brown and no longer pink. Taste it for seasonings and add a touch more salt, if desired. Set aside.

CONTINUED NEXT PAGE >

Fresh Pork Sausages CONTINUED

Remove blade on meat grinder and fit machine with sausage-filling tube. Using 1 intestine at a time, fit onto sausage filling tube. Tie end of intestine into a knot and using a fine pin, poke end a few times. Load sausage grinder with pork mixture and turn machine on. Once meat starts to fill the end, slowly guide the intestine along with the meat, keeping it slow and steady. Fill the intestine until it is filled almost to the end and stop the machine. Remove sausage link and tie off the end. You can coil the sausage or make links by pinching points of the link at the length of sausages you want. Repeat with remaining meat and intestines.

Gently prick the sausages with pin and pack the sausages in resealable plastic bags and refrigerate for up to 3 days or freeze for up to 6 months.

MAKES ABOUT 8 LB (3.5 KG) SAUSAGE LINKS.

Drying the sausage: If you want to dry the sausages you can hang them up in your cantina. The cantina, like a root cellar, is a cold storage room or cellar, usually under the front porch. The room keeps cool in the summer and very cold in winter. It is perfect for curing salami or storing tomato sauce and other preserves. The sausages will need to be watched carefully and not get too cold or they will not cure properly. Be sure to check on them! They usually take a good 6 to 8 weeks or more to dry properly.

Sausage Kabobs *Spiedini di Salsiccia*

We love sausages at our house. Quick and easy, these kabobs make a great weeknight meal. The zucchini and tomatoes add juiciness and flavour to the sausage. To serve, slide everything off the skewer and enjoy it with the toasted bread—a crunch of Italian-style taste.

1 sprig fresh rosemary

½ cup (125 mL) extra virgin olive oil

4 fresh Italian sausages (mild or hot), about 1 lb (450 g)

1 cup (250 mL) grape tomatoes

1 zucchini, cut into ½-inch (1 cm) chunks

2 Tbsp (30 mL) chopped fresh Italian parsley

3 cloves garlic, minced

¼ tsp (1 mL) salt

¼ tsp (1 mL) pepper

6 slices Italian bread

REMOVE LEAVES FROM ROSEMARY and place in a small saucepan. Add oil to saucepan and heat oil over medium-low heat until rosemary begins to become fragrant and lose colour. Remove from heat and let stand for 10 minutes.

Meanwhile, slice each sausage into 6 pieces each. Skewer onto metal or soaked wooden skewers, alternating with zucchini and cherry tomatoes. Set aside.

> Soak wooden skewers in warm water in shallow dish for about 30 minutes before using. Soaking helps prevent flare-ups on the grill.

Preheat grill to medium-high heat.

Remove rosemary leaves from oil and add parsley, garlic, salt and pepper to oil. Set half of oil mixture aside. Place kabobs on greased grill for about 12 minutes, basting with remaining oil and turning occasionally until no longer pink inside and vegetables are golden.

Brush bread slices with remaining oil and grill, turning once, for about 4 minutes or until golden brown and crisp. Serve with kabobs.

MAKES 4 SERVINGS.

Polenta with Sausage and Rapini
Polenta con Salsiccia e Rapini

As comforting as mashed potatoes, polenta fills your tummy with warmth and nutrition. The cornmeal is cooked until smooth and thick, then topped with garlic-spiked rapini. Sausage makes this a hearty dinner.

1 cup (250 mL) water
1 bunch rapini, trimmed and coarsely chopped
2 Tbsp (25 mL) extra virgin olive oil
2 Italian sausages, casings removed
4 cloves garlic, minced
¼ tsp (1 mL) hot pepper flakes
¼ tsp (1 mL) salt

Polenta
4 cups (1 L) Chicken Stock (see recipe p. 22)
1 cup (250 mL) cornmeal
½ cup (125 mL) water
⅓ cup (80 mL) freshly grated Parmigiano Reggiano cheese
2 Tbsp (30 mL) chopped fresh Italian parsley
Shaved Parmigiano Reggiano cheese (to taste)

BRING WATER TO A BOIL in a large non-stick skillet. Add rapini, cover and steam for about 7 minutes, stirring occasionally or until tender. Drain well and set aside.

Return skillet to medium heat and add oil. Cook sausage, breaking up with spoon, for about 6 minutes or until no longer pink inside. Add rapini, garlic, hot pepper flakes and salt; cook for 5 minutes or until beginning to turn golden.

Polenta: Bring stock to a boil in saucepan and gradually whisk in cornmeal. Bring to a gentle simmer, stirring frequently, for about 12 minutes or until polenta mounds on spoon. Stir in water to loosen slightly. Stir in cheese and parsley until cheese is melted.

Spoon polenta into shallow soup bowls and top with rapini and sausage mixture. Sprinkle with shaved Parmesan, if desired.

> For a more casual presentation, you can stir the rapini and sausage mixture into the polenta before serving.

MAKES 4 SERVINGS.

Nonna Ortenzia's Meatballs *Polpette di Nonna Ortenzia*

My Nonna and mother can make some pretty mean meatballs. Cooking with them taught me how to recreate their delicious family favourite meatballs. These are moist and tasty just like my Nana's; we use Nana in our family when we talk about my Nonna. It's a term of endearment that has always stuck around. I've made them for friends and family and they just love them!

8 oz (250 g) ground veal or beef

8 oz (250 g) ground pork

½ cup (125 mL) fresh bread crumbs

1 egg

2 Tbsp (30 mL) finely chopped fresh Italian
   parsley

2 Tbsp (30 mL) grated Parmesan cheese

1 clove garlic, minced

½ tsp (2 mL) salt

Pinch of hot pepper flakes

1 batch Homemade Tomato Sauce
   (see recipe p. 23)

If you don't have fresh bread crumbs, soak some stale bread in milk or water and break up into small pieces and add to meat mixture.

You can substitute 3 to 4 cups (750 mL to 1 L) of store bought tomato or pasta sauce for this recipe.

PREHEAT OVEN TO 350°F (180°C). Line a baking sheet with foil.

In a large bowl, mix together veal, pork, bread crumbs, egg, parsley, Parmesan, garlic, salt and red pepper flakes until well combined. Using wet hands roll meat mixture into 1-inch (2.5 cm) balls. Place on prepared baking sheet.

Bake in oven for about 12 minutes or until no longer pink inside, but not browned.

Meanwhile, heat pasta sauce over medium heat. Add meatballs to sauce and simmer gently for about 10 minutes. Serve with pasta or in a bun.

MAKES 24 MEATBALLS.

Red Pepper and Prosciutto Stuffed Pork Roast

Porchetta Ripiena di Peperoni Rossi e Prosciutto

We use a lot of pork in our house. It starts early in the year with making fresh sausages and then continues as it's the centre of special occasions and simple meals.

Pork roasts are a wonderful dish to feed a crowd. They are lean and soak up all the flavour they are given. Having visited many pork farms, I often think that I would have liked to be a pork farmer, but for now I am happy to support local farmers. I will stick to cooking!

2 Tbsp (30 mL) extra virgin olive oil
1 small onion, finely chopped
2 cloves garlic, minced
4 oz (125 g) prosciutto, finely chopped
2 tsp (10 mL) dried oregano
1 cup (250 mL) chopped roasted red peppers
½ cup (125 mL) fresh bread crumbs
2 Tbsp (30 mL) chopped fresh Italian parsley
½ tsp (2 mL) salt
½ tsp (2 mL) pepper
1 2 lb (1 kg) boneless centre cut pork roast
2 Tbsp (30 mL) Dijon mustard

You can buy roasted red peppers in jars or roast your own (see recipe p. 26).

IN A SKILLET, heat oil over medium-high heat and cook onion, garlic, prosciutto and oregano for about 5 minutes or until onions are softened and prosciutto is crisp. Add peppers, bread crumbs, parsley, salt and pepper. Remove from heat and set aside.

Preheat oven to 325°F (160°C).

Using a sharp chef's knife, start cutting pork loin lengthwise in a spiral fashion to "unroll" the loin until you end up with 1 long rectangle piece. Using a meat mallet, pound out pork to an even thickness. Spread with mustard and the prepared filling, leaving a 1 inch (2.5 cm) border at 1 short end. From other end start rolling up pork loin, as if it were a jelly roll.

Using kitchen string, tie the pork loin to secure at 2-inch (5 cm) intervals. Place in roasting pan and roast in oven for about 1 hour or until a meat thermometer registers 155°F (70°C).

Let stand for 10 minutes before slicing.

MAKES 8 SERVINGS.

Roast Pork and Potatoes *Porchetta con Patate*

This is a great meal to share with family and friends to enjoy local farm offerings. I've included the rabbit variation as we ate a lot of rabbit growing up. We had a hutch in the backyard so I could play with the bunnies when they were small. Knowing we took good care of them and fed them well made a lasting impression. Farmers do their jobs well and their products reflect that.

⅓ cup (80 mL) chopped parsley

6 cloves garlic, minced

3 Tbsp (45 mL) grated Parmesan cheese

5 Tbsp (75 mL) extra virgin olive oil, divided

One 3 lb (1.5 kg) bone-in pork rib or loin roast

2 lb (1 kg) yellow fleshed potatoes (about 8), cut into wedges

1 tsp (5 mL) salt

½ tsp (2 mL) fresh ground pepper

IN A BOWL, mix together parsley, garlic, cheese and 3 Tbsp (45 mL) of the oil. Rub mixture all over roast and place in a large roasting pan.

Toss potatoes with remaining oil, salt and pepper and spread around roast in pan. Roast in oven for about 1 hour and 45 minutes or until thermometer inserted in centre of roast reaches 155°F (70°C) and a hint of pink remains inside.

Remove roast to cutting board and let stand for 5 minutes before slicing. Sprinkle potatoes with Parmesan cheese before serving.

MAKES 8 SERVINGS.

Rabbit Variation (see photo): Omit pork and use 1 fresh rabbit, cut into pieces. Toss rabbit pieces with parsley mixture and brown in skillet. Place in roasting pan, add ½ cup (125 mL) white wine over rabbit. Roast with potatoes for about 1 hour or until meat and potatoes are tender.

If the rabbit is sold whole, ask the butcher to cut it into 6 or 8 pieces for you to get started quickly on the recipe.

Roast Pork *Porchetta*

Traditionally, in parts of Italy, porchetta is a suckling pig that is cooked on a spit over an open fire, sliced up and sold on street corners in buns for a tasty lunch. You can also roast the pork with potatoes underneath to absorb all its delicious juices. This is the perfect dinner for any special occasion. We served porchetta and pork roast for all my kid's baptisms and it has become a tradition to share that delicious flavour on other occasions now, too. Sometimes I think I make this just for the sandwiches we get from the leftovers!

1 4 lb (1.8 kg) boneless pork loin roast
½ cup (125 mL) chopped fresh Italian parsley
4 cloves garlic, minced
4 large fresh sage leaves, minced
2 Tbsp (30 mL) minced fresh basil leaves
2 Tbsp (30 mL) grated Romano cheese
1 Tbsp (15 mL) minced fresh rosemary
1 tsp (5 mL) salt
½ tsp (2 mL) pepper
⅓ cup (80 mL) extra virgin olive oil, divided

Four large sage leaves chopped is approximately 2 Tbsp (30 mL). You can substitute 1 Tbsp (15 mL) dried sage leaves for the fresh.

PREHEAT OVEN TO 350°F (180°C).

Using a sharp chef's knife, cut pork loin almost all the way through and open the cut roast like a book. Cut both sides again to open up flat and set aside.

In a bowl, stir together parsley, garlic, sage, basil, cheese, rosemary, salt and pepper. Add half of the oil and stir to combine. Spread half of the herb mixture over inside of pork roast and roll back up. Tie with string to secure and rub remaining herb mixture all over roast.

Place porchetta in a roasting pan and roast in bottom third of oven for about 2 hours, turning occasionally until golden brown all over and thermometer inserted in centre of roast reaches 160°F (71°C). Drizzle with remaining oil and cover with foil. Let stand for 10 minutes before slicing.

Uncover and place on cutting board. Remove strings and slice thinly.

MAKES 8 TO 10 SERVINGS.

Veal Roast Stuffed with Figs

Arrosto di Vitello con Ficchi

I love serving veal for special occasions; you can prepare it ahead of time and roast it when you need it. Be sure to order a veal roast ahead of time as they can sometimes be difficult to find.

1 pkg (250 g) dried figs, chopped
1½ cups (375 mL) dry red wine
1 boneless veal loin or shoulder roast
  (about 2 lb / 1 kg)
1 tsp (5 mL) dried thyme
½ tsp (2 mL) dried oregano
¼ tsp (1 mL) salt
¼ tsp (1 mL) pepper
1 cup (250 mL) beef broth
1 Tbsp (15 mL) Dijon mustard

You will need 1½ cups (375 mL) chopped dried figs for this recipe if you can't find the package. Look for figs in either the produce aisle or baking supplies in grocery stores.

IN A SAUCEPAN, bring figs and wine to a boil. Reduce heat, cover and simmer for about 5 minutes or until figs are very tender. Remove figs to a plate with a slotted spoon leaving wine in the saucepan; let figs cool slightly.

Using a sharp knife, cut the roast in half lengthwise almost all the way through and open it up like a book. Repeat on both sides of the roast.

Preheat oven to 375°F (190°C). Using a meat mallet, pound roast to flatten it; set aside.

In a small bowl, combine thyme, oregano, salt and pepper. Sprinkle over inside and outside of roast. Place figs along centre of roast and roll up jelly-roll style. Tie roast with string to secure. Place on a rack in a small roasting pan.

Roast in oven for about 1 hour and 10 minutes or until just a hint of pink remains and juices run clear. Meanwhile, add beef broth to reserved wine and bring to boil. Boil for about 10 minutes or until reduced by half. Whisk in mustard.

Remove strings from roast and slice into 1-inch (2.5 cm) thick slices. Spoon wine sauce over top.

MAKES 6 SERVINGS.

Pork Option: You can substitute 2 pork tenderloins (about 2 lb / 1 kg total) for the veal roast. The pork tenderloins will take about 20 minutes in the oven.

Veal Cutlets with Homemade Tomato Sauce

Cotolette di Vitello con Sugo

This is a great recipe for entertaining. You can freeze these cutlets in sauce and save them for a cold night to warm everyone's hearts. The leftovers—if there are any—make great sandwiches the next day!

¼ cup (60 mL) all-purpose flour

½ tsp (2 mL) salt, divided

½ tsp (2 mL) pepper, divided

1 egg

3 Tbsp (45 mL) water

¾ cup (190 mL) dried Italian seasoned
   bread crumbs

4 Tbsp (60 mL) grated Parmesan or Romano
   cheese, divided

1 tsp (5 mL) dried oregano

1 lb (450 g) veal scallopini cutlets

¼ cup (60 mL) extra virgin olive oil (approx.)

1 batch Homemade Tomato Sauce (see
   recipe p. 23)

Scallopini is thinly sliced meat like a cutlet. It is usually veal, but it can also be prepared with other meats, such as turkey or beef. If none are available you can make your own from a larger cut of meat by slicing it thinly.

IN A SHALLOW BOWL, combine flour and half each of the salt and pepper. In another shallow bowl, whisk egg with water. In a third shallow bowl, combine bread crumbs, 2 Tbsp (30 mL) cheese and oregano.

Sprinkle remaining salt and pepper over veal. Dredge each cutlet in flour, then place into egg bowl, letting excess drip off. Coat evenly with breadcrumb mixture. Place on waxed paper-lined baking sheet.

Preheat oven to 350°F (180°C).

In a large non-stick skillet, heat oil over medium-high heat. Cook cutlets in batches turning once for about 3 minutes or until light golden. Add more oil if necessary.

Ladle some of the tomato sauce into a large shallow baking dish. Top with cutlets, overlapping slightly. Ladle more of the sauce over top. Sprinkle with remaining Parmesan cheese. Cover with foil and bake in oven for about 30 minutes or until sauce is bubbly and veal is no longer pink inside and very tender.

MAKES 4 SERVINGS.

Make ahead: You can cover and refrigerate breaded cutlets for up to 4 hours before pan frying.

Garlic Thyme Sliced Steak with Arugula

Tagliata all'Aglio e Timo con Rucola

Celebrating friend's birthdays is always something I enjoy doing and making their favourite dishes with Italian twists has become a bit of a habit. Here, fresh herbs and garlic make
thick juicy steaks a new Italian favourite.

3 Tbsp (45 mL) red wine vinegar

1 Tbsp (15 mL) extra virgin olive oil

4 cloves garlic, minced

2 Tbsp (30 mL) chopped fresh thyme

1 Tbsp (15 mL) chopped fresh oregano

1 Tbsp (15 mL) Dijon mustard

4 boneless rib-eye steaks ——————————— *When picking steaks they should be about 1 inch (2.5 cm) thick.*

3 Tbsp (45 mL) lemon juice

1 container (5 oz / 150 g) baby arugula ——————— *You will need 8 cups (2 L) of baby arugula.*

½ cup (125 mL) shaved Parmesan cheese

Pinch of salt

Pinch of pepper

A few strips lemon zest (for garnish) ——————— *If you like lemon flavour you can add as much lemon zest as you like, a few wisps on each serving will do though.*

IN A SHALLOW HEAT-PROOF GLASS DISH, stir together vinegar, oil, garlic, thyme, oregano
and mustard. Add steaks and turn to coat. Let stand for 10 minutes.

Place steaks in pan and cook, turning once for about 10 minutes or desired doneness.
Remove steaks to cutting board and let stand for 3 minutes. Cut steaks into slices.

Return pan to medium heat and add lemon juice; heat through. Spread arugula into
a large bowl and then drizzle with heated lemon juice. Sprinkle with Parmesan and top
with sliced steak. Season with salt and pepper before serving. Garnish with lemon zest, if
desired.

MAKES 8 SERVINGS.

You can also grill these steaks and drizzle the lemon juice overtop of the dish. Simply grill over high heat to sear; reduce heat to medium-high and grill to your desired level of doneness. Let them rest before slicing.

VEGETABLES AND SALADS

The convenience of having fresh fruit and vegetables in your own backyard is something that many Italians either have or remember. The gardens I remember as a kid took up for space than the houses that they surrounded. I loved running out into my family's garden and plucking fresh carrots from the earth or sitting in the soil eating fresh peas still warm from the sun. As I got older, I started realizing the importance of what else was in that garden: tomatoes, garlic, onions, potatoes, apples, pears, plums and cherries, to name a few. No matter where we lived or what size of backyard we had, there was always a garden.

For many years, we had a pear tree in our backyard that produced an overwhelming number of pears. Even after we had sent many home with friends and relatives, we still had more than we needed. This forced me to come up with many recipes for pears, some of which you will find in this book.

My dad always made me happy by taking home some of the pears that weren't quite ripe. He would simply boil the pears in a pot until tender. It's such a simple way to use up pears and enjoy their flavour easily and with little fuss. Simply boiling them helped keep them longer and gave them a different texture—a new twist on how to use up pears.

Back then and now, tomatoes and herbs are a huge part of our backyard garden. Tomatoes should be fresh and ripe enough to slice for a sandwich, chop into a salad or make into a sauce. The addition of fresh herbs to any of these makes a great combination. On a good year, there are even some tomatoes and herbs to tuck into the freezer for later in the year. Fresh herbs are a great addition to any recipe. Picking a few basil leaves for tomato sauce or a sprig of rosemary for the potatoes makes a difference in creating some spectacular dishes.

My parents have always grown lots of peppers, including hot ones, and tomatoes of all sizes. I particularly love the sweet grape tomatoes for popping into my mouth like candy. Most of the time, they never make it into the kitchen!

Ask your family what they want to plant next year and make it a new tradition that will inspire everyone to get in the kitchen. The fruit of your labour is as inspiring as it is delicious when you get to enjoy it with your family.

Garlicky Green Beans *Fagiolini con Aglio*

Green beans are a favourite of mine, especially the long flat beans that I would help my Nonna pick from the garden. When it came time to pick the beans it was a game to see who had the longest. I think Nonna let me win each time.

3 lb (1.5 kg) green beans, trimmed
¼ cup (60 mL) extra virgin olive oil
4 cloves garlic, minced
¼ cup (60 mL) chopped fresh parsley
  or mint
¼ tsp (1 mL) salt
¼ tsp (1 mL) pepper

You can make a delicious salad with any of the leftover beans. Simply drizzle with red wine vinegar once they are cold and enjoy. You may want to add a sprinkle of fresh mint to brighten it up.

IN A LARGE SAUCEPAN OF BOILING WATER, cook green beans for 5–8 minutes or until tender but still slightly crisp; drain well.

In a large saucepan or skillet, heat oil over medium heat. Cook garlic, stirring often, for 1 minute. Add beans and toss to coat. Cover and cook, tossing twice, for about 8 minutes or until hot. Add parsley, salt and pepper; toss to coat.

MAKES 12 SERVINGS.

Make ahead: Once you have boiled and drained the beans, chill the beans under cold running water; drain well. Wrap in towel and place in a plastic bag; refrigerate for up to 24 hours.

Baked Greens *Verdura al Forno*

If you are overrun with greens in your garden, here is a great recipe that I created to use a lot up. It is perfect to enjoy alongside meats or with pasta. Any leftovers are tasty as a soup base with beans for a vegetarian meal.

1 head broccoli

1 head escarole

Half a head of green cabbage

5 Tbsp (75 mL) extra virgin olive oil

½ cup (125 mL) chopped green onions

3 cloves garlic, minced

1 tsp (5 mL) hot pepper flakes

3 Tbsp (45 mL) chopped Italian parsley

2 tsp (10 mL) salt

1 cup (250 mL) fresh bread crumbs

¼ cup (60 mL) grated Parmesan cheese

To make fresh bread crumbs use fresh bread slices or buns and tear them up into a food processor and pulse until crumbs form. Any extra can be frozen.

CUT BROCCOLI into small florets. Peel stem and cut into small pieces. Chop escarole and cabbage coarsely.

In a pot of boiling water, boil broccoli, escarole and cabbage in batches, if necessary, for about 3 minutes or until tender crisp. Drain well and set aside.

Preheat oven to 400°F.

In a large non-stick skillet, heat 3 Tbsp (45 mL) oil over medium heat. Add greens, onions, garlic, salt and hot pepper flakes. Cook, stirring often, for 8 minutes or until tender. Remove from heat and stir in parsley and salt. Spoon into a greased casserole dish.

Sprinkle with bread crumbs and cheese. Drizzle with remaining oil and bake for about 10 minutes or until golden.

MAKES 8 TO 10 SERVINGS.

Make ahead: Prepare the casserole, cover and refrigerate for up to 2 days. Bake in a 350°F (180°C) oven for about 30 minutes or until heated through.

Eggplant "Meatballs" *Polpette di Melanzane*

I ate these almost every day while in Italy a few years back visiting family. These little eggplant "meatballs" can be made ahead, frozen and then reheated to serve at another meal. Make smaller ones for a new appetizer idea or larger ones with a drizzle of pasta sauce for a great vegetarian meal.

2 large or 4 small eggplants, about 4 lb
   (2 kg) total
2 eggs
2 cups (500 mL) dry seasoned bread
   crumbs (approx.)
⅔ cup (160 mL) freshly grated Parmigiano
   Reggiano cheese

2 cloves garlic, minced
2 Tbsp (30 mL) chopped fresh basil
2 Tbsp (30 mL) chopped Italian parsley
½ tsp (2 mL) salt

LINE BAKING SHEET WITH PARCHMENT PAPER; set aside.

Trim ends from eggplant and cut eggplant into chunks.

In a large pot of boiling water over medium-high heat, cook eggplant for about 20 minutes or until soft. (Let a single piece cool slightly and test the eggplant between your fingers.) Drain well and let cool slightly. Gently squeeze eggplant to remove some of the moisture in the eggplant. Place in a large bowl.

Preheat oven to 400°F (200°C).

Add eggs, bread crumbs, cheese, garlic, basil, parsley and salt to the cooked eggplant. Mix together using your hands to form a soft mixture. Start making small oval shapes using about ½ cup (125 mL) of the mixture. Coat "meatballs" in more bread crumbs and place on prepared baking sheet. Bake in oven for about 30 minutes, turning once or until golden brown on both sides.

> *You can also pan-fry the "meatballs" in oil for about 5 minutes per side or until golden instead of baking them.*

MAKES 24 "MEATBALLS."

Make ahead: Once cooked, let meatballs cool and refrigerate in a covered dish for up to 5 days. To freeze, pack meatballs into airtight container and layer with waxed paper if necessary. Freeze for up to 1 month. Thaw in refrigerator overnight and reheat in a shallow casserole dish with pasta sauce. Cover and bake in 350°F (180°C) oven for about 20 minutes or until heated through.

Roast Potatoes *Patate al Forno*

Roasting the potatoes at a high heat and not turning them to get that golden colour and crisp texture was one of the first tips I recall my Godfather, Ortenzio Sicoli, giving me. This is a side dish that is served often at our house because it goes so well with any protein and is a hit with kids. Golden brown and crisp potatoes are combined with fresh herb flavour; serve alongside any main dish or on their own.

2 lb (1 kg) yellow-fleshed potatoes
3 Tbsp (45 mL) extra virgin olive oil
1 Tbsp (15 mL) chopped fresh rosemary
1 Tbsp (15 mL) chopped fresh thyme

1 Tbsp (15 mL) chopped fresh basil
½ tsp (2 mL) salt
½ tsp (2 mL) pepper

PREHEAT OVEN TO 425°F (220°C). Line baking sheet with parchment paper.

Cut potatoes into 1-inch (2.5 cm) chunks; place in large bowl. Toss with oil, rosemary, thyme, basil, salt and pepper.

Spread potatoes onto prepared pan in single layer. Roast for 45–60 minutes or until browned and tender.

MAKES 4 TO 6 SERVINGS.

Sprinkle with some freshly grated Parmesan cheese before serving for an added flavour boost.

Grilled Polenta with Asparagus and Mushrooms

Polenta Grigliata con Asparagi e Funghi

You can make the polenta a day ahead and store it in the refrigerator. Simply cut and grill as directed in the recipe. If your barbecue is large enough, grill the vegetables alongside the polenta. I love serving this after heading to the market or farm to pick up local asparagus and mushrooms. It makes a wonderful dinner or part of an antipasto.

Polenta

4 cups (1 L) water

1 cup (250 mL) cornmeal

½ cup (125 mL) grated Parmesan cheese

3 Tbsp (45 mL) chopped fresh Italian parsley

½ tsp (2 mL) salt

¼ tsp (1 mL) pepper

⅓ cup (80 mL) extra virgin olive oil, divided

3 Tbsp (45 mL) aged balsamic vinegar

2 cloves garlic, minced

½ tsp (2 mL) salt

Pinch of hot pepper flakes

1 bunch fresh asparagus, trimmed

1 lb (450 g) oyster mushrooms, tough stems trimmed

⅓ cup (80 mL) shredded Asiago cheese

Fresh small basil leaves

> Hold asparagus spears near end and snap off about 1 inch (2.5 cm) of the tough stems. If you hold them too close to the top you will lose a lot of great tasting asparagus. You can use a knife instead if you wish to make the bottoms uniform.

> 1 lb (450 g) of oyster mushrooms is about 4 cups (1 L).

Polenta: In a deep large saucepan, bring water to a boil. Whisk in cornmeal until combined. Using a wooden spoon, stir frequently for about 15 minutes or until it is very thick and mounds onto a spoon. Stir in cheese, parsley, salt and pepper. Scrape into greased 11 × 7-inch (28 × 18 cm) baking dish. Refrigerate for about 1 hour or until room temperature.

Preheat grill to medium-high heat.

CONTINUED NEXT PAGE >

Grilled Polenta with Asparagus and Mushrooms CONTINUED

Meanwhile, in a large bowl, whisk together ¼ cup (60 mL) oil, vinegar, garlic, salt and hot pepper flakes. Add asparagus and mushrooms. Toss to coat.

Cut cold polenta into 6 squares and brush both sides with remaining oil. Place on a grill over medium-high heat for about 10 minutes, turning once, or until golden brown. Remove to a platter.

Place asparagus and mushrooms on grill over medium-high heat for about 10 minutes, turning occasionally or until golden brown and asparagus is tender-crisp. Return to bowl and toss with vinegar mixture. Divide asparagus and mushrooms among polenta squares and drizzle with any remaining vinegar mixture.

Sprinkle with Asiago cheese and garnish with basil.

MAKES 6 SERVINGS.

Mixed Green Salad *Insalata Verde Mista*

With the bite of radicchio and the smoothness of romaine, this tart little salad is great for finishing off a meal. Having homemade red wine vinegar is great but store-bought works just fine. As a kid I would wait until the last bit of salad was eaten before tipping the bowl of vinegar dressing into my mouth to drink. This dressing is that good!

5 cups (1.25 L) torn romaine leaves

1 small head radicchio, torn

2 cups (500 mL) torn Boston lettuce leaves, arugula or spinach

1 carrot, grated

⅓ cup (80 mL) extra virgin olive oil

¼ cup (60 mL) red wine vinegar

Pinch of dried oregano

Salt, to taste

Pepper, to taste

You can substitute mesclun or spring mix leaves, if available, for the romaine, radicchio and Boston lettuce. 1 small radicchio will give you about 2–3 cups (500–750 mL) torn and you will need about half a head of Boston lettuce.

IN A LARGE BOWL, toss together romaine, radicchio, Boston lettuce and carrot.

In a small bowl, whisk together oil, vinegar, oregano, salt and pepper. Toss with the salad.

MAKES 6 TO 8 SERVINGS.

Tomato Cucumber Salad *Insalata di Pomodoro e Cetriolo*

I love serving Fresine (see recipe p. 101) with this salad. Once most of the tomato and cucumber is eaten, break up the Fresine and let it soak up all the tasty vinegar dressing. This is perfect to add to a weeknight meal. Using in-season, hearty plum tomatoes adds lots of flavour and prevents a soupy salad, if you don't want to soak it up with Fresine.

4 plum tomatoes
1 English cucumber
Half a small sweet onion, thinly sliced
  (optional)
3 Tbsp (45 mL) extra virgin olive oil
3 Tbsp (45 mL) red or white wine vinegar
1 tsp (5 mL) dried oregano
1 tsp (5 mL) salt
¼ tsp (1 mL) fresh ground pepper

You can use field cucumbers, but scrape out the seeds before slicing.

REMOVE CORES FROM TOMATOES and cut into chunks. Place in a large bowl. Cut cucumber in half lengthwise; cut into slices. Add to bowl along with onion.

In a small bowl, whisk together oil, vinegar, oregano, salt and pepper. Pour over salad and toss to coat.

MAKES 4 SERVINGS.

Tomato and Pine Nut Salad

Insalata di Pomodoro e Pinoli

Tomatoes can overflow in gardens and should not be forgotten. They can be enjoyed in many different ways and can add sweetness to salads and sauces. Look for red, orange and yellow tomatoes in stores or pick them fresh from your garden to create a rainbow of flavour in this colourful salad. Use any interesting tomato variety in this dish, like candy stripe or sweet green. Whatever you use, this salad is a great addition to serve up with other antipasti or as an end to dinner.

4 tomatoes, such as beefsteak or heirloom
   varieties (red, yellow and orange)
¾ tsp (4 mL) salt, divided
¼ tsp (1 mL) fresh ground pepper, divided
¼ cup (60 mL) extra virgin olive oil
1 Tbsp (15 mL) Balsamic Glaze (see recipe p. 93)
1 small clove garlic, minced
1 cup (250 mL) halved grape tomatoes
   (yellow or red)
⅓ cup (80 mL) pine nuts, toasted
2 Tbsp (30 mL) chopped fresh basil
1 Tbsp (15 mL) chopped fresh Italian parsley
3 oz (90 g) Gorgonzola or Asiago cheese,
   crumbled

To toast pine nuts, place them in a dry non-stick skillet over medium heat and stir constantly for about 5 minutes or until light golden. Alternatively, place them on a baking sheet and toast them in a 350°F (180°C) oven for about 8 minutes, shaking pan once.

Freeze Gorgonzola for about 15 minutes for easier crumbling.

SLICE TOMATOES INTO ½-INCH (6 mm) thick slices and arrange decoratively on a platter, overlapping slightly if necessary. Sprinkle tomatoes with ¼ tsp (1 mL) of the salt and a pinch of pepper.

In small bowl, whisk together oil, Balsamic Glaze, garlic and ¼ tsp (1 mL) salt; set aside.

In another bowl, stir together grape tomatoes, pine nuts, basil, parsley and remaining salt and pepper. Spoon over sliced tomatoes. Spoon vinegar mixture over tomatoes and sprinkle with cheese.

MAKES 8 SERVINGS.

Make ahead: Make salad, cover and refrigerate for up to 4 hours. Bring to room temperature before serving.

Mixed Pepper and Bocconcini Pasta Salad

Insalata di Pasta con Peperoni Misti e Bocconcini

Toasting the pasta gives it a nutty flavour and adds golden colour to this salad. I love making this for family gatherings and I always make extra to pack up for lunches the next day. Toss in some chopped salami or cooked chicken and it's a meal in a bowl.

1 cup (250 mL) baby shells or baby bowtie
    pasta

1 large red pepper

1 large yellow pepper

1 large green pepper

Half a bunch of asparagus, trimmed

2 Tbsp (30 mL) extra virgin olive oil, divided

1 can (19 oz / 540 mL) artichoke hearts,
    drained and chopped

1 tub (7 oz / 200 g) mini bocconcini, drained

3 Tbsp (45 mL) aged balsamic vinegar

2 Tbsp (30 mL) basil or sundried tomato
    pesto

¼ tsp (1 mL) salt

Pinch of pepper

⅓ cup (80 mL) chopped, pitted oil-cured
    olives (optional)

You could also use about 3/4 cup (190 mL) orzo for this salad instead of the small pasta.

You will need 6 to 8 artichoke hearts if a can is unavailable.

You can substitute 1 1/3 cups (325 mL) chopped bocconcini or fresh mozzarella for the mini bocconcini.

IN SMALL NON-STICK SKILLET, toast pasta, stirring often over medium-high heat for about 2 minutes or until golden brown. Remove from heat.

In saucepan of boiling, salted water, cook pasta for about 8 minutes or until *al dente*. Drain well and rinse under cold water; place in a large bowl.

Cut peppers into quarters; place in a large bowl with asparagus. Toss with 1 Tbsp (15 mL) oil. Place on a greased grill over medium-high heat and grill for about 8 minutes, turning once or twice until golden and tender but crisp. Remove to cutting board and chop; add to pasta. Stir in artichoke hearts and boconccini.

In a small bowl, whisk together balsamic vinegar and remaining oil, pesto, salt and pepper. Drizzle over pasta mixture and toss to combine. Sprinkle with olives, if using.

MAKES 8 SERVINGS.

Make ahead: This salad will keep covered in the refrigerator for up to 2 days.

Pickled Hot Peppers *Peperoncino Sottaceto*

There is always a point in the meal where my dad asks for hot peppers. I always have hot pepper flakes on hand. At his house, he enjoys these zingy hot peppers added to many dishes. These pack a punch, but are great served with cheeses, pastas or chopped up into salads with tomatoes and Fresine (see recipe p. 101). You can use a variety of fresh hot peppers in this mix if you like; jalapeno, cherry red or scotch bonnets are just a few to consider.

8 oz (225 g) small hot peppers (green
   and red)
1 Tbsp (15 mL) salt
1–2 cups (250–500 mL) white vinegar
½–1 cup (125–250 mL) canola oil

The amount of vinegar and oil will vary depending on the bowl size you use as well as the jar size you choose to store them in.

WASH THE PEPPERS WELL and trim off the stems. Slice into thin rings and place in a bowl. Scrape up any seeds and place them into the bowl as well.

Be sure to use gloves when slicing the hot peppers especially if you are sensitive to heat.

Sprinkle salt over peppers and toss to coat well. Place a small plate over top to press down on the peppers and refrigerate for 24 hours.

Drain off any liquid from peppers. Pour vinegar overtop of peppers to cover, enough to cover them. Cover with plastic wrap and refrigerate for 12–24 hours. Drain peppers well and pack into small resealable jars or containers. Cover with oil and top with lid. Refrigerate for up to 2 months.

MAKES 1 CUP (250 ML).

Pickled Pepper Mix *Peperoni Misti Sottaceto*

These peppers have an *agrodolce* flavour, which is sweet and tangy. That makes them perfect for porchetta and other meat sandwiches. They are also delicious on their own or on an antipasto platter. Better yet, add some to a pasta dish for added zip.

1 red bell pepper, sliced
1 yellow bell pepper, sliced
1 orange bell peppers, sliced
1 cup (250 mL) white vinegar
1 cup (250 mL) water
3 Tbsp (45 mL) sugar

1 Tbsp (15 mL) salt
½ tsp (2 mL) hot pepper flakes
2 cloves garlic, minced
2 Tbsp (30 mL) chopped fresh Italian
  parsley

IN A LARGE SAUCEPAN, bring peppers, vinegar, water, sugar, salt and hot pepper flakes to a boil. Remove from heat and stir in garlic and parsley. Cover and let stand until cooled to room temperature. Pack in airtight container with lid and refrigerate for up to 1 month.

MAKES 3 CUPS (750 ML).

Pickled Peppers, Mushrooms and Onions

Peperoncini, Funghi e Cipolle

Here is another mix that is perfect to serve alongside meats or on their own with some fresh bread. These vegetables are tasty, simple and easy.

1 Tbsp (15 mL) extra virgin olive oil
1 sweet onion, sliced
8 oz (225 g) mushrooms, sliced ——————
2 cloves garlic, minced
1 cup (250 mL) pickled pepperoncini ——————
   peppers, stems removed
1 Tbsp (15 mL) Worcestershire sauce
¼ tsp (1 mL) salt
¼ tsp (1 mL) pepper

If you buy mushrooms in bulk you will need 2 cups (500 mL).

Look for pickled pepperoncini in the pickle aisle of the grocery store. They are typically a whole little green pepper with a stem on them.

IN A NON-STICK SKILLET, heat oil over medium-high heat and saute onion, mushrooms and garlic for 8 minutes or until softened and golden. Remove from heat and stir in pepperoncini peppers, Worcestershire, salt and pepper. Let cool slightly before serving.

MAKES 3 CUPS (750 ML).

Pumpkin Flower Fritters *Fiore di Zucca Fritti*

You can make a couple batches of this batter if you have a lot of flowers. Have some fun and enjoy them on their own or with this pesto mayo. A little drizzle of balsamic or red wine vinegar is also a great flavour combination.

1 cup (250 mL) all-purpose flour
3 Tbsp (45 mL) chopped fresh herbs
2 tsp (10 mL) baking powder
¾ tsp (4 mL) salt
1 cup (250 mL) sparkling water
1 cup (250 mL) canola oil (approx.)
10–12 fresh pumpkin flowers, stamens
  removed

You can use any combination of fresh herbs you like, or all of one. Use milder herbs such as parsley, mint and basil.

Pesto Mayo
¼ cup (60 mL) light mayonnaise
4 tsp (20 mL) basil pesto

IN A BOWL, whisk together flour, herbs, baking powder and salt. Pour in water, whisking until it's the consistency of thick pancake batter.

Pour enough oil to fill bottom of a large non-stick skillet and heat over medium-high heat.

Using your fingers, gently dip flowers into the batter to coat well and let excess drip off. Place in skillet (be careful do not crowd the pan). Let cook for a few minutes until the batter starts to set and almost bubble around the edges. Carefully turn over and cook until light golden brown. Remove to a paper towel-lined plate and repeat with remaining flowers.

Pesto Mayo: In a small bowl, whisk together mayonnaise and pesto. Serve with fritters.

MAKES 10 TO 12 FRITTERS.

Make ahead: If you want to make fritters ahead, fry and let them drain well on a paper towel; refrigerate when they are cool. Place on a baking sheet in a 350°F (180°C) oven for 15 minutes or until they are crisp.

DESSERTS

When my family gets all in a tizzy about someone having a baby or married, it's not because we are happy for them really—it's because we get to cook and bake for them! I'm kidding, we really are happy for them, but Italians show their love and caring through food and lots of it.

For my bridal shower, it was fabulous to have all of my friends and family in the hall but the dessert was what everyone was waiting for. I love how my aunts offered to make cookies for sweet trays; their generosity is always outpouring. Of course we never have enough room in our stomachs for all of those treats so wrapping them up in napkins and tucking them into our purses is pretty common. Now that people have become food savvy, they've realized that all that hard work can get crushed by a wallet in those purses. They will leave containers by the sweets table for tucking away goodies.

With more and more wedding showers being attended by both men and women, I think the sweets table will always be popular. However, perhaps there is still a need for groups of women to get together. Events like those are always a great place to exchange recipes, find out who is cooking what and who is putting which herbs in their *conserba* ("sauce").

Hard Honey Biscuits *Mostaccioli*

In Italy, these cookies are made into different shapes: fish, baskets, ladies, horses and much more. They are typically sold at outdoor markets, especially during Patron Saint festivals.

These are a hard textured cookie and are great to dip into coffee or slowly chew on to get the flavour. I enjoyed small pieces as a young child before I had teeth and loved every minute of it. How do I remember so well, you ask? My parents have reminded me and my own children enjoyed them the same way.

This recipe is adapted from Comare Carmella Berardelli, my sister's Godmother, and is soft and easy to roll out. She likes to cut the dough on an angle so each piece comes out like a diamond shape.

1 jar (500 g) liquid honey
2 eggs
5 cups (1.25 L) all-purpose flour (approx.)
1¼ tsp (6 mL) baking soda
¼ cup (60 mL) sliced almonds

You will need about 2 cups (500 mL) of liquid honey for this recipe.

PREHEAT OVEN TO 350°F (180°C). Line 2 baking sheets with parchment paper; set aside.

In a large stand mixer or bowl, beat honey and eggs together.

In another bowl, whisk together flour and baking soda. Gradually add flour mixture to honey mixture until combined. Add almonds until distributed evenly. Scrape onto a floured work surface and knead gently to make sure everything is blended well and dough is soft, not sticky.

Roll out dough into thick narrow ropes, about 1 inch (2.5 cm) in width and 24 inches (60 cm) in length. Pat down slightly and cut into about 2-inch (5 cm) diamond shapes. Place on prepared baking sheets and bake for about 12 minutes or until light golden brown. Let cool completely.

MAKES 6 DOZEN COOKIES.

Keep in airtight containers at room temperature for up to 2 weeks or frozen for up to 2 months.

Little Old Ladies *Vecchiarelle*

These honey fritters are tasty and sweet, making them the perfect ending to any meal. In the south of Italy, there are stories that say the name of these fritters came from the *vecchiarelle*—"little old ladies"—that made them in the town. With a hint of spice and almonds, they have a delicious flavour that is perfect with espresso.

½ cup (125 mL) sugar, divided

½ cup (125 mL) warm water

1 Tbsp (15 mL) active dry yeast

1¾ cups (435 mL) all-purpose flour

⅓ cup (80 mL) toasted almonds, finely chopped

¼ tsp (1 mL) ground cinnamon

Pinch of ground cloves

Pinch of salt

4 cups (1 L) canola oil

1 cup (250 mL) liquid honey

IN A LARGE BOWL, dissolve ½ tsp (2 mL) of the sugar into water. Sprinkle with yeast and let stand for about 10 minutes or until frothy. Stir in flour, almonds, cinnamon, cloves, salt and remaining sugar to form a ragged dough. Turn out onto a floured surface and knead until smooth dough forms. Cover and let rise for about 1 hour or until doubled in size.

On a floured surface, knead dough and roll it out to a generous ½-inch (1 cm) thick rectangle. Cut into about 24 finger-length pieces.

Meanwhile, in a large deep heavy saucepan or deep fryer, heat oil to 365°F (185°C). Fry fritters 4 or 5 at a time, turning over once, for about 2–4 minutes or until golden brown. Remove to a paper towel-lined baking sheet.

In another large saucepan, heat honey over medium heat. Add half of the fritters and toss to coat them with honey. Scoop out with a slotted spoon onto a serving platter and repeat with remaining fritters.

MAKES 24 FRITTERS.

Zia Peppina's Tiramisu *Tiramisu di Zia Peppina*

Everyone loves Zia Peppina's Tiramisu! My dad's oldest sister has been like a mom to so many in our family. It has been a much loved dessert in our family for a long time. I was so happy when she shared the recipe with me, while I watched her make it. It truly is everyone's favourite dessert during holiday time, but it's great any time of year! Not using the mascarpone cuts down on the cost, but definitely not the flavour.

1½ cups (375 mL) espresso or strong
    black coffee

⅓ cup (80 mL) coffee, brandy or
    nut liqueur

1 pkg (500 g) savioardi cookies

1 batch Lemon Cream, just made (still warm)
    (see recipe p. 197)

2 Tbsp (30 mL) unsweetened cocoa
    powder or shaved dark chocolate

Look for savioardi or ladyfinger cookies in Italian delis or grocery stores. Many larger grocery stores carry them year round but they may be more prevalent during the Christmas season.

To shave chocolate, you can grate a piece of dark chocolate over top of the tiramisu, or substitute chocolate sauce and gold flakes for a super fancy plated dessert.

IN A BOWL, combine coffee and liqueur. Quickly dip each savioardi cookie into coffee mixture and start placing cookies in a greased 13 × 9-inch (33 × 23 cm) baking dish, continue with cookies to cover bottom.

Pour half of the lemon cream over top of the cookie layer. Lay another cookie layer on top of cream. Drizzle any remaining coffee-liqueur mixture overtop of cookies. Spread layer with remaining cream. Sprinkle evenly with cocoa.

Refrigerate for at least 2 hours or until cookies are softened and cream is set. Overnight is best. You can cover with plastic wrap and refrigerate for up to 3 days. Good luck trying to keep it that long!

MAKES 8 TO 10 SERVINGS.

Amaretti Chocolate Custard with Raspberries

Crema al Cioccolato con Amaretti e Lamponi

I remember my Nonna making chocolate pudding. What a wonder it was! She used this box of powder she had found at the grocery store that her friends had told her about. I loved it and would bother my mother for it often. As I got older, my tastes changed and as much as I loved that chocolate pudding, I wanted a bit more. This recipe is dedicated to those tasty boxes of pudding but is made for adult tastes. It is well suited for special occasions as it is both rich and delicious. This custard is jazzed up with the crunch of amaretti cookies and a hit of fresh fruit.

8 eggs
¼ cup (60 mL) unsweetened cocoa
  powder
¾ cup (190 mL) sugar
4 cups (1 L) 2% milk, at room temperature
2 Tbsp (30 mL) Amaretto liqueur
¾ cup (190 mL) crushed Amaretti cookies
  (see recipe p. 214)
4 oz (125 g) chopped bittersweet chocolate
1 cup (250 mL) fresh raspberries
½ cup (125 mL) toasted sliced almonds

If you don't want to make your own Amaretti, you can buy store bought versions in Italian stores or the cookie aisle of larger grocery stores.

PREHEAT OVEN TO 325°F (160°C).

In a large bowl, whisk together eggs, cocoa powder and sugar until combined. Slowly whisk in milk and liqueur until smooth. Add cookies and whisk until well distributed.

Pour mixture into ten ¾ cup (190 mL) or twelve ½ cup (125 mL) greased ramekins or custard cups and set in large baking pan. Fill pan with hot water halfway up sides of the ramekins. Bake for about 20 minutes or until firm on top but still slightly jiggly in centre. Let cool.

Meanwhile, setup a double boiler to melt the chocolate in a heatproof bowl over hot, but not boiling water. Drizzle over each custard and serve sprinkled with raspberries and almonds.

MAKES 10 TO 12 SERVINGS.

Lemon Cream *Crema al Limone*

This versatile cream is what Zia Peppina, my dad's oldest sister, uses in her tiramisu. Once I made it, I found other great uses for it like filling my Peach Cookies (see recipe p. 225) and as a filling for any cake. As my good friend Jesse Lauzon suggested, it is also great as a doughnut filling! This would work well to fill cannoli shells (the puff pastry ones) that my family usually calls horns. It's so delicious and creamy that, to be frank, it's just as good with a spoon!

4 cups (1 L) 2% milk

8 egg yolks

½ cup (125 mL) sugar

½ cup (125 mL) all-purpose flour

Four 2-inch (5 cm) strips of lemon zest

IN A SMALL SAUCEPAN or microwaveable bowl, heat milk for about 5 minutes or until steaming. (This will only take a couple of minutes in the microwave)

Meanwhile, in a heatproof bowl, stir together egg yolks, sugar and flour. Gradually stir in hot milk, changing over to a whisk after adding about half of the milk. Setup a double boiler with the bowl by placing it over a saucepan of hot (not boiling) water. Stir in lemon zest. Cook while stirring for 15–30 minutes or until thickened to the consistency of pudding.

Pour cream through a fine mesh sieve into another bowl to remove any lumps and lemon zest. Use right away for recipes such as Zia Peppina's Tiramisu (see recipe p. 194) or a trifle. Cover directly with plastic wrap and chill until firm for recipes such as Peach Cookies or as a filling for cakes or doughnuts.

MAKES 4 CUPS (1 L).

You can serve this as a delicious pudding on its own. It serves 6 to 8 people; sprinkle with a few berries or drizzle it with melted chocolate before serving.

Jam Tart *Crostata di Marmellata*

I ate this a number of times during my stay in Italy. This recipe happens to be adapted from my cousin Marisa, from my dad's side of the family. She filled it with homemade prune jam. You can use your favourite type of jam, but it's best is to use a chunky home-made jam with lots of fruit for great fruit flavour. The crust softens as it sits but it just gets richer in flavour. If it isn't eaten quickly, it could last for about 5 days.

½ cup (125 mL) butter, softened
½ cup (125 mL) sugar
2 eggs
½ tsp (2 mL) vanilla
2¼ cups (560 mL) all-purpose flour
⅓ cup (80 mL) toasted hazelnuts, finely
   chopped
½ tsp (2 mL) baking powder
Pinch of salt
1½ cups (375 mL) fruit jam (homemade,
   if possible)

You can substitute a vanilla-infused baking powder for the baking powder and vanilla. You can find it in the baking aisle in little envelopes; simply use about half an envelope.

IN A LARGE BOWL, beat butter with sugar until fluffy. Beat in eggs, one at a time, beating well after each addition. Beat in vanilla.

In another bowl, whisk together flour, hazelnuts, baking powder and salt. Add to butter mixture and stir to form dough. Divide dough into two-thirds for the bottom crust and one-third for the top crust. Wrap in plastic wrap and refrigerate for at least 30 minutes or for up to 1 day.

Preheat oven to 350°F (180°C).

On a floured surface roll out the larger disk of dough to fit an 11-inch (28 cm) tart tin with a removable bottom. Spread jam into crust. Roll out remaining dough and cut into 1-inch (2.5 cm) thick strips. Weave strips to create a latticed top. Pinch ends together and trim to fit the pan. Bake for about 45 minutes or until golden and filling is bubbly.

The jam will look like it doesn't fill the tart but as it bakes it will rise beautifully and look amazing!

MAKES 12 SERVINGS.

You can also dust this tart with icing sugar if desired or brush the top with an apricot jam for a glazed crostata.

Apple and Pear Hazelnut Strudel
Strudel di Mela, Pera e Nocciola

I had apple and pear trees that were fruitful and offered up more fruit then I needed so I decided to have fun in the kitchen by creating and sharing recipes with family and friends. I loved Zia Lina's, my dad's middle sister's, apple pie filling, so one day I got her to show me how she came up with it. Her secret is a touch of Frangelico! I changed things up a bit and decided to add some pears to create this tasty strudel. You can use this filling in your favourite pie crust, too; it's just as delicious! Serve with vanilla ice cream or my dad's and my son Nicolas's favourite ice cream—chocolate.

3 apples, peeled and sliced

3 pears, peeled and sliced

2 Tbsp (30 mL) lemon juice

3 Tbsp (45 mL) + ½ cup (125 mL) butter

¼ cup (60 mL) packed brown sugar

2 Tbsp (30 mL) sugar

3 Tbsp (45 mL) all-purpose flour

Pinch of salt

½ cup (125 mL) dried cranberries

2 Tbsp (30 mL) Frangelico or other hazelnut liqueur

⅓ cup (80 mL) toasted hazelnuts, finely chopped

10 sheets phyllo pastry

Apples like Granny Smith or Northern Spy are perfect to use for this recipe. For pears, I like to use Bartlett pears.

It is best to thaw the phyllo pastry in the refrigerator overnight.

IN A LARGE BOWL, toss apples and pears with lemon juice.

In a large non-stick skillet, melt 3 Tbsp (45 mL) butter over medium-high heat; cook apples, pears and sugars for about 8 minutes or until softened. Add flour and salt and cook for another 2 minutes or until thickened. Remove from heat.

Meanwhile, in a small bowl combine cranberries and liqueur; let stand for 2 minutes. Add cranberries to apple and pear mixture; let cool slightly. Divide nuts into 9 equal piles.

Preheat oven to 400°F (200°C). Line baking sheet with parchment paper; set aside.

Melt remaining butter. Brush 1 sheet of phyllo with some of the butter; sprinkle with 1 pile of the nuts. Repeat with 4 more sheets of phyllo and nuts. Place the top long edge of the fifth sheet of phyllo in the middle of buttered phyllo to extend the length of the phyllo. Brush with butter and sprinkle with nuts. Repeat with remaining phyllo and nuts.

Spread fruit mixture on phyllo leaving 2 inches (5 cm) of space along one of the longer sides and short ends. Fold over and tuck in sides and continue to roll up. Brush with remaining butter and gently place on a prepared baking sheet. Using a serrated knife make slits in top of the strudel.

Bake in centre of oven for about 20 minutes or until golden brown.

MAKES 8 SERVINGS.

Ice Cream Roll Cake *Rotolo al Gelato*

For summer birthdays—or whenever you want cake and ice cream—Zia Lina's cake is the one you need! When we visited when I was just a kid, she always seemed to have a slice in the freezer for me. This can last in the freezer for up to 2 weeks and is perfect for all seasons. You can make it more than once using different ice creams, fill it with your favourite curd or use whipped cream and strawberries. The fillings are endless!

4 eggs, separated
¼ cup (60 mL) water
¾ cup (190 mL) sugar, divided
1 tsp (5 mL) vanilla
¼ tsp (1 mL) cream of tartar
½ cup (125 mL) all-purpose flour
¼ cup (60 mL) cornstarch
¼ tsp (1 mL) baking powder
2 tsp (10 mL) icing sugar
6 cups (1.5 L) Neapolitan ice cream, softened

Let the ice cream stand in the refrigerator for about 30 minutes to soften or at room temperature for about 15 minutes. Be sure to stir it well before using to make sure the consistency is the same throughout.

PREHEAT OVEN TO 400°F (200°C). Line a 17 × 11-inch (43 × 28 cm) baking sheet with parchment paper. Grease and dust with flour; set aside.

In a bowl, beat egg yolks with water until pale. Beat in ½ cup (125 mL) of the sugar until thickened; beat in vanilla.

In another bowl, beat egg whites with cream of tartar until foamy. Beat in remaining sugar until stiff peaks form; fold into yolk mixture. Sift together flour, cornstarch and baking powder; fold into egg mixture.

Spread batter into prepared pan evenly and bake for 15 minutes or until light golden and firm. Let cool in pan for 5 minutes.

Sprinkle a large clean tea towel with some icing sugar. Run knife around the edges of pan and invert cake onto tea towel. Carefully remove parchment paper. Using towel as a guide, roll up starting from one of the shorter sides; jelly-roll style and set-aside until cool.

Unroll cake and spread with ice cream. Roll back up and place on a large platter; cover and freeze for at least 6 hours or until frozen solid. Sprinkle with icing sugar before slicing.

MAKES 12 TO 16 SERVINGS.

You can sprinkle a bit of your favourite liqueur onto the cake before spreading on the ice cream, if desired. You can also drizzle the outside with melted bittersweet chocolate for a little hit of chocolate.

Celebration Custard Cake *Torta di Crema per Celebrazione*

For my parents' 40th wedding anniversary my sister converted all their 8-mm home movies into DVDs to make it easier for our family to enjoy. While we were watching, we noticed how often food was in the movies and how every occasion had a cake. I remember those cakes like it was yesterday and I remember that I loved every bite. How could you not? It was a soft light cake with layers of chocolate and vanilla custard, topped with a light whipped cream. No one had a recipe for it; we always went to the local bakery to pick one up.

I did my own research and practiced making the cake for several family gatherings and came up with a recipe that everyone enjoyed. This cake has now appeared in my children's lives and I can't wait to continue making it and enjoying the cake's appearance in new family movies we create for the future.

Vanilla Custard

2 cups (500 mL) 1% milk
⅓ cup (80 mL) all-purpose flour
½ cup (125 mL) sugar
Pinch of salt
2 eggs
2 tsp (10 mL) vanilla

Chocolate Custard

2 cups (500 mL) 1% milk
⅓ cup (80 mL) all-purpose flour
⅓ cup (80 mL) sugar
Pinch of salt
2 eggs
3½ oz (100 g) semi-sweet chocolate
2 tsp (10 mL) vanilla

Cake Layers

8 eggs
1⅓ cups (325 mL) sugar, divided
1⅓ cups (325 mL) all-purpose flour
⅓ cup (80 mL) water
Pinch of salt
½ tsp (2 mL) cream of tartar
½ cup (125 mL) rum, divided

Whipped Cream

3 cups (750 mL) 35% whipping cream
½ cup (125 mL) icing sugar

Vanilla Custard: In a saucepan, whisk together milk and flour and cook over medium heat until smooth. Whisk in sugar and salt and cook, whisking, for about 5 minutes or until mixture comes to a boil. Remove from heat.

In a small bowl, whisk eggs. Pour in about half of the hot mixture and whisk to combine. Return egg mixture into saucepan and whisk over medium heat until it returns to just boiling. Remove from heat and whisk in vanilla. Pour into a bowl and cover surface with plastic wrap. Refrigerate for 2 hours or until cold and firm.

CONTINUED NEXT PAGE >

Celebration Custard Cake CONTINUED

Chocolate Custard: In a saucepan, whisk together milk and flour and cook over medium heat until smooth. Whisk in sugar and salt and cook, whisking, for about 5 minutes or until mixture comes to a boil. Remove from heat.

In a small bowl, whisk eggs. Pour in about half of the hot milk mixture and whisk to combine. Return egg mixture into saucepan and whisk over medium heat until it returns to just boiling. Remove from heat and whisk in chocolate and vanilla until smooth. Pour into a bowl and cover surface with plastic wrap. Refrigerate for 2 hours or until cold and firm.

Cake Layers: Preheat oven to 350°F (180°C). Line two 18 × 13-inch (45 × 33 cm) baking sheets with parchment paper; set aside.

Separate egg yolks from egg whites. Beat egg yolks with an electric mixer for about 5 minutes or until thickened. Beat in 1 cup (250 mL) of the sugar slowly until eggs feel smooth between your fingers.

Stir together flour and salt. Fold 3 equal additions of flour into egg mixture, alternating with 2 additions of the water, half each time.

In another bowl, beat egg whites until foamy and beat in cream of tartar until soft peaks form. Beat in remaining sugar until stiff peaks form. Fold in one-third of the egg whites into egg yolk mixture to lighten. Add remaining egg whites and fold until no streaks remain.

Divide batter among prepared baking sheets. Spread evenly with offset spatula. Bake in top and bottom third of oven, switching halfway through, for about 15 minutes or until light golden and set. Remove from oven and let cool.

Cut cakes in half horizontally. Place 1 layer onto a large platter or cake board. Drizzle with one-third of the rum. Spread with half of the chocolate custard evenly over top. Top with another layer of cake. Drizzle with another third of rum. Spread vanilla custard over top. Top with another cake layer. Drizzle with remaining rum and chocolate custard. Top with last cake layer. Refrigerate cake for 15 minutes, while you make the whipped cream.

Whipped Cream: In a large bowl, whip cream and icing sugar until stiff. Spread evenly over sides and top of cake. Use a piping bag filled with cream to make decorative designs, if desired.

Cake can be refrigerated for up to 2 days.

MAKES 24 SERVINGS.

Chocolate Hazelnut Cornmeal Cake

Torta di Polenta alla Nocciola e Cioccolato

Balsamic vinegar was not something I grew up with but red vinegar was a staple in my family's home and still is. However, I couldn't let a vinegar that is so good slip past me— so I added it to a dessert! Chocolate cake has always been a favourite for so many family members, so I took their favourite flavour and made a gluten-free option with chocolatey taste and texture that even non-chocolate lovers enjoy.

1 cup (250 mL) water

¼ cup (60 mL) cornmeal

⅓ cup (80 mL) ground hazelnuts

6 oz (180 g) bittersweet chocolate, chopped

⅓ cup (80 mL) unsalted butter, cubed

3 eggs, separated

⅔ cup (160 mL) sugar, divided

1 tsp (5 mL) vanilla

3 Tbsp (45 mL) aged balsamic vinegar

1 Tbsp (15 mL) icing sugar

1 Tbsp (15 mL) Frangelico or other hazelnut liqueur

Chocolate or vanilla ice cream (optional)

PREHEAT OVEN TO 350°F (180°C). Line bottom of a 9-inch (23 cm) springform pan with parchment paper and set aside.

In a small saucepan, bring water to a boil. Whisk in cornmeal and cook, stirring for about 5 minutes or until thickened and starting to become smooth. Stir in hazelnuts and cook for 1 minute. Place the mixture in a large bowl.

Add chocolate and butter and stir until both are melted and smooth; set aside.

Divide egg yolks and egg whites into 2 separate bowls. Using an electric hand mixer, beat egg yolks with half of the sugar and vanilla until pale yellow in colour. Clean beaters thoroughly and beat egg whites with remaining sugar until stiff, but not dry, peaks form. Stir egg yolk mixture into cornmeal mixture until combined. Fold egg whites into mixture until no streaks remain. Scrape batter into prepared pan. Bake for about 35 minutes or until set. Let cool slightly.

In a bowl, whisk together vinegar, remaining sugar and liqueur. Using a skewer or toothpick, poke cake all over. Pour vinegar mixture all over cake and let cake cool completely.

Cut cake into wedges and serve with ice cream, if desired.

MAKES 16 SERVINGS.

Almond Variation: Omit ground hazelnuts and hazelnut liqueur and substitute with ground almonds and amaretto.

COOKIES

When I was young, I wasn't allowed to stay at home by myself when my parents went out to visit. I never minded because I actually enjoyed visiting my parent's friends and other relatives. I was one of the only kids around at the time so it was fun to get the attention and have a platter of sweets all to myself while my parents enjoyed espresso and adult conversation.

All of that attention didn't last forever as eventually my sister and cousins were born. Being the oldest, I loved going for coffee and visiting people, even if I didn't get quite the attention that I was used to.

When little ones were around, we would play together and watch TV, sneaking into the kitchen to grab a snack that seemed to be strategically placed for us to find. We never minded digging into those snacks and the adults certainly didn't mind us running into the kitchen while they sat comfortably enjoying their conversations and coffee. Somehow a glass of milk or juice would appear for us as if someone was anticipating our next moves.

I remember my dad would pick up the phone and say something like, *"Ok, veniemu fra pocco per nu cahao."* ("Ok, we will be there shortly for a coffee."). I knew that meant we were heading out soon for a visit. I loved visiting my aunts and cousins and my Nonni. It was a time when technology was simple so listening to a record player and watching some television was all we'd have available as entertainment. Enjoying the company of others was truly the best part.

This is something my family is doing again. While the kids are playing around us and coming in to grab a snack or treats, I enjoy having friends and family come over to chat and catch up. Although these days, the kids are playing video games in between sneaking in to grab that last cookie.

Tie Plates *Pizzelle*

My Nonna, aunts and cousins have been playing around with this recipe for thin snowflake-shaped cookies for years during the holiday season. Massive quantities of these cookies are made to fulfill the needs of many Christmas appetites. I adjusted this recipe to make a more moderate quantity, so if you're trying them out it won't be as intimidating. You will need an electric pizzelle maker which looks like a waffle iron except much flatter. I tried making them in my waffle iron but it was too thick and didn't get the very thin snowflake look to them. You can also find older non-electric pizzelle irons in some antique shops. A perfect gift for the foodie that has everything!

5 eggs
¾ cup (190 mL) sugar
½ cup (125 mL) canola oil
1 tsp (5 mL) anise or vanilla extract

1¾ cups (435 mL) all-purpose flour (approx.)
2 tsp (10 mL) baking powder

IN A LARGE BOWL, whisk eggs until frothy. Whisk in sugar until dissolved. Whisk in oil and extract. Stir together flour and baking powder and whisk 1 cup (250 mL) into the liquid mixture. Stir in remaining flour mixture until a smooth and sticky dough forms. It will be thick and pasty; if necessary add more flour to reach desired consistency, 1 Tbsp (15 mL) at a time.

Heat your pizzelle iron and spray with a cooking spray or brush with oil or butter. Drop 1 Tbsp (15 mL) of the batter into the centre of each pizzelle shape. Close lid and seal with latch. Let cook for about 1 minute or until very light golden. Remove from plates and lie flat on top of each other. Repeat with remaining batter. Enjoy warm or cold. They will crisp as they cool.

> If you want to shape the pizzelle remove them quickly from the plate and roll them into a cone shape or place them into a small bowl to create a cup shape. To fill them with a Kit Kat bar, break the bar into the 4 segments and place one in hot pizzelle and then roll up with it and place seam side down to cool.

MAKES 30 PIZZELLE COOKIES.

> Once cooled you can store the cookies in an airtight container or resealable bag for at least 2 weeks. I don't put them in the freezer because they are so thin they will shatter and break apart.

Nutella Tie Plates *Pizzelle di Nutella*

I could eat Nutella with pretty much anything, so when I tried this recipe, I fell in love. These cookies are light and airy with that thin tasty texture only a pizzelle can give you. I serve these up with more Nutella spread overtop and a sprinkle of diced strawberries and icing sugar. No one will be able to resist.

3 eggs
¾ cup (190 mL) sugar
½ cup (125 mL) butter, melted
½ cup (125 mL) Nutella or other hazelnut-
    chocolate spread

2 Tbsp (30 mL) vanilla
2¼ cups (560 mL) all-purpose flour
2 tsp (10 mL) baking powder
½ tsp (2 mL) instant coffee or espresso
    powder (optional)

IN A LARGE BOWL, whisk together eggs, sugar and butter until light and well combined. Whisk in Nutella and vanilla.

Add flour, baking powder and instant coffee, if using, and stir well until a sticky dough forms.

Heat your pizzelle iron and spray with cooking spray or brush with oil or butter. Drop 1 Tbsp (15 mL) of the batter in centre of each pizzelle shape. Close lid and seal with latch. Let cook for about 1 minute or until very light golden. Remove from plates and lie flat on top of each other. Repeat with remaining batter.

> I like to have 2 forks handy to help gently lift off the pizzelle cookies. Using cooking spray helps keep it well greased so that they don't stick to the iron. If you have any that break, enjoy them as is, stir them into ice cream or crush them and add them to some whipped cream or yogurt for a special treat.

MAKES 2 DOZEN COOKIES.

Mom's Super Yummy Pan Cookies

Biscotti di Mamma Deliziosi Fatti alla "Landia"

When we had bake sales at school, all the kids would bring Italian cookies. I wanted my mom, Giustina, to make something a little different and these were what she came up with. They were always a hit! They are almost better than chocolate chip cookies. This cookie is one giant cookie at the start. But of course you need to cut it into pieces to share. I've changed the recipe slightly and I think it's still one of my favourites. You can use extra melted white chocolate to drizzle over the bars before serving. They are tasty on their own but even more tantalizing with ice cream. Yum!

1 cup (250 mL) butter, softened

¾ cup (190 mL) sugar

¾ cup (190 mL) packed brown sugar

2 eggs

1 Tbsp (15 mL) vanilla

1 tsp (5 mL) instant coffee granules or
instant espresso powder (optional)

2¼ cups (560 mL) all-purpose flour

1 tsp (5 mL) baking soda

½ tsp (2 mL) salt

2 cups (500 mL) milk chocolate chips

1 cup (250 mL) white chocolate chips

½ cup (125 mL) chopped hazelnuts

PREHEAT OVEN TO 375°F (190°C). Line a 15 × 10-inch (38 × 25 cm) baking sheet with parchment paper; set aside.

In a large bowl, beat butter and sugars until fluffy. Beat in eggs one at a time, beating well after each addition. Add the coffee granules, if using, to the vanilla and stir. Beat into butter mixture.

In another bowl, whisk together flour, baking soda and salt. Gradually stir flour mixture into butter mixture until combined. Add milk and white chocolate chips and hazelnuts and stir to combine.

Spread batter onto prepared baking sheet, using floured hands to press evenly. Bake in oven for about 25 minutes or until golden brown. Let cool slightly. Remove to cutting board and cut into 48 bars.

> If you don't press it all down to the edges of the pan and let it cook until it's just light golden brown, about 20 minutes, they will be soft and brownie like, another way to enjoy them. Let cool completely and place in airtight container in the freezer for up to 2 months.

MAKES 48 BARS.

Amaretti Cookies *Amaretti*

These are great little crunchy cookies that are ideal for dunking into coffee although they are just as good for munching on their own. They are a wonderful addition to a table of sweets.

2 cups (500 mL) unblanched whole almonds
2 egg whites
1 cup (250 mL) sugar
2 Tbsp (30 mL) all-purpose flour
1 Tbsp (15 mL) almond extract
1 tsp (5 mL) baking powder
1 tsp (5 mL) icing sugar (optional)

You can substitute hazelnuts for the almonds in these cookies.

PREHEAT OVEN TO 350°F (180°C). Line 2 baking sheets with parchment paper; set aside.

In a food processor, chop almonds until in small pieces with some powdery granules. Set aside.

In a large bowl, beat egg whites until soft peaks form. Gradually beat in sugar, until ribbons fall from beaters when lifted. Stir in almonds, flour, almond extract and baking powder.

Do not use dark baking sheets for these cookies as they cause over browning.

Drop level tablespoons or small ice cream scoops of batter, about 2 inches (5 cm) apart on prepared baking sheets. Using your fingertips, shape each into a neat circle.

Bake in centre of oven for about 12 minutes or until cookies are light brown and crisp on top. Set pans on a cooling rack and let cool for 2 minutes. Transfer cookies to rack and let cool completely. Sprinkle with icing sugar, if desired.

Try dipping them in melted chocolate for a new twist on these crisp bites.

MAKES 40 COOKIES.

Can be stored at room temperature for about 2 weeks or frozen for up to 1 month.

Chocolate Mostaccioli *Mostaccioli Cioccolati*

These cookies are what we eat each year for the celebration of Saint Anthony of Abbot on January 17. They are delicious during the Christmas holiday season as well, so you can make extra at Christmastime and freeze them for the upcoming Saint Anthony celebration. My paternal Nonno was named Antonio so I was honoured to include Anthony in my son's name. These cookies are served at a celebration that is a true testament to names in our family and their meanings. They are not just for Saints but also for remembering family members.

1½ cups (375 mL) blanched whole
  almonds
½ cup (125 mL) liquid honey
¾ cup (190 mL) unsweetened cocoa
⅔ cup (160 mL) granulated sugar

2 tsp (10 mL) orange zest
½ tsp (2 mL) cinnamon
½ tsp (2 mL) ground cloves
¼ cup (60 mL) brewed espresso coffee
¾ cup (190 mL) all-purpose flour (approx.)

PREHEAT OVEN TO 375°F (190°C). Line baking sheet with parchment paper; set aside.

Place almonds in a food processor and grind to a fine powder. Add honey, cocoa, sugar, orange zest, cinnamon, cloves and espresso and pulse to combine. Add flour, ¼ cup (60 mL) at a time, until dough forms a ball. Remove to floured surface and knead dough, adding up to ¼ cup (60 mL) more flour, until a smooth dough forms; the dough should not be sticky.

Divide dough in half and roll out each half to a 12 × 12-inch (30 × 30 cm) square. Cut into 2-inch (5 cm) squares. Place cookies on prepared baking sheet.

Bake in oven for about 9 minutes or until set. Repeat with remaining dough.

MAKES 6 DOZEN COOKIES.

Store in an airtight container for up to 2 weeks or freeze for up to 2 months.

Almond Biscotti *Biscotti di Mandorle*

You can't go wrong with a classic and these are perfect for dipping in coffee. As a young child I would sneak up onto Nonno's lap and dunk my biscotti into his coffee. Why not my dad's, you ask? That answer is easy—Nonno put milk and sugar in his coffee!

1¾ cups (435 mL) all-purpose flour
2 tsp (10 mL) baking powder
¾ cup (190 mL) unblanched whole
  almonds
2 eggs
¾ cup (190 mL) granulated sugar

⅓ cup (80 mL) butter, melted
2 tsp (10 mL) vanilla
½ tsp (2 mL) almond extract
1½ tsp (7 mL) orange zest
1 lightly beaten egg white

PREHEAT OVEN TO 350°F (180°C). Line baking sheet with parchment paper; set aside.

In a large bowl, combine flour, baking powder and almonds.

In a separate bowl, whisk together eggs, sugar, butter, vanilla, almond extract and orange zest; stir into flour mixture until a soft, sticky dough forms. With floured hands, transfer dough to a lightly floured work surface; divide dough in half.

Roll each dough half into a 12-inch (30 cm) long log. Transfer to prepared baking sheet.

Brush tops with egg white. Bake for 20 minutes or until firm when touched. Remove from oven and let pan cool on rack for 5 minutes. Transfer each log to cutting board. Cut diagonally into ¾-inch (2 cm) thick slices. Stand cookies upright on baking sheet; bake for another 20–25 minutes or until golden. Let cool on rack.

MAKES 2 DOZEN BISCOTTI.

Store in an airtight container for up to 2 weeks or freeze for up to 2 months.

Hazelnut and Anise Biscotti

Biscotti di Nocciola all'Anice

Biscotti are traditional Italian cookies made with little fat—only eggs are used to give them richness. Aniseed adds a distinct sweet licorice flavour.

1 cup + 2 Tbsp (280 mL) all-purpose flour	2 eggs
½ tsp (2 mL) baking soda	⅓ cup (80 mL) granulated sugar
½ tsp (2 mL) anise seeds, crushed	1 tsp (5 mL) vanilla
½ cup (125 mL) chopped hazelnuts or almonds	1 lightly beaten egg white
	2 tsp (10 mL) coarse sugar

PREHEAT OVEN TO 350°F (180°C). Line baking sheet with parchment; set aside.

In a large bowl, combine flour, baking soda, aniseed and hazelnuts or almonds.

In a separate bowl, whisk together eggs, sugar and vanilla; stir into flour mixture until a soft sticky dough forms.

With floured hands, transfer dough to a lightly floured surface; divide dough in half. Place dough on prepared baking sheet and shape each dough half into 8 × 2-inch (20 × 5 cm) rectangles. Brush with egg white and sprinkle with sugar.

Bake in oven for about 15 minutes or until light golden. Remove from oven; let cool for about 20 minutes. Transfer to a cutting board and cut diagonally into ½-inch (1 cm) thick slices. Reduce oven temperature to 300°F (140°C).

Stand slices upright on baking sheet and return to oven and bake for about 20 minutes or until golden and dry. Let cool on rack.

MAKES 2 DOZEN BISCOTTI.

Store in an airtight container for up to 2 weeks or freeze for up to 2 months.

Christmas Biscotti: Omit nuts and use ½ cup (125 mL) each red and green candied cherries, chopped.

My Mother's Chocolate Almond Biscotti

Biscotti al Cioccolata e Mandorla di Mamma

These simple and easy to make biscotti are jazzed up with more chocolate than you can imagine. It is a great one to keep in the cookie jar and pull out to enjoy with espresso or a big glass of milk.

¼ cup (60 mL) butter, softened

½ cup (125 mL) sugar

2 eggs

1 Tbsp (15 mL) vanilla

½ cup (125 mL) unsweetened cocoa powder

1½ cups (375 mL) all-purpose flour, divided

2 tsp (10 mL) baking powder

Pinch of salt

½ cup (125 mL) mini chocolate chips

½ cup (125 mL) toasted almonds, slivered or chopped

6 oz (180 g) semisweet chocolate, chopped

PREHEAT OVEN TO 350°F (180°C). Line baking sheet with parchment paper; set aside.

In a large bowl, beat butter and sugar until fluffy. Beat in eggs, one at a time. Beat in vanilla. Beat in cocoa, 1 cup (250 mL) of the flour, baking powder and salt. Stir in remaining flour, mini chocolate chips and almonds.

With floured hands, shape into 2 logs about 10 inches (25 cm) long and place onto prepared baking sheet. Flatten slightly to form a rectangle.

Bake in oven for about 20 minutes or until firm. Reduce heat of oven to 300°F (150°C). Let biscotti cool in pan on rack for about 15 minutes. Using a serrated knife, cut diagonally into ½-inch (1 cm) slices. Place on a baking sheet, cut side down. Bake in oven for about 15 minutes, turning once or until crisp. Let cool completely.

Meanwhile, in a bowl set over hot (not boiling) water, melt chocolate until smooth. Dip half of each biscotti into the chocolate or drizzle biscotti with chocolate. Refrigerate until chocolate is firm.

MAKES 2 DOZEN BISCOTTI.

Store in an airtight container for up to 2 weeks or freeze for up to 2 months.

Hazelnut Chocolate–Filled Cookies

Biscotti Ripieni di Nutella

Here is an easy sandwich cookie that is made special with the addition of hazelnut chocolate spread. If you want, you can use melted chocolate instead.

½ cup (125 mL) butter, softened
½ cup (125 mL) sugar
2 eggs
½ tsp (2 mL) vanilla
2¼ cups (560 mL) all-purpose flour
⅓ cup (80 mL) toasted hazelnuts, finely
    chopped
½ tsp (2 mL) baking powder
Pinch of salt
Nutella or other hazelnut-chocolate spread
Hazelnut halves (optional), 1 per cookie

I don't call for an amount of Nutella in the recipe because it changes depending on how much you want in the cookie. If you have a small jar of Nutella it will be plenty, but if you love it like I do, you may just want to pick the biggest jar you can find!

IN A LARGE BOWL, beat butter with sugar until fluffy. Beat in eggs, one at a time beating well after each addition. Beat in vanilla.

In another bowl, whisk together flour, hazelnuts, baking powder and salt. Add to butter mixture and stir to form dough. Divide dough into 2 discs. Wrap each in plastic wrap and refrigerate for at least 30 minutes or up to 1 day.

Preheat oven to 350°F (180°C). Line baking sheets with parchment paper; set aside.

On a floured surface, roll dough to ¼-inch (6 mm) thickness. Cut out circles using cookie cutter and place on baking sheet. Bake in oven for about 12 minutes or until golden. Let cool completely.

Spread half of the cookies with the chocolate spread and top with remaining cookies. Spread a small amount of chocolate spread on top and top with a hazelnut half, if desired.

MAKES 3 DOZEN COOKIES.

You can freeze the cookies before filling them with the hazelnut-chocolate spread. Freeze in airtight container for up to 1 month. When desired, defrost and spread as instructed.

Shrimp Cookies *Biscotti "Gamberetti"*

These cookies don't have an ounce of shrimp in them but guess what shape they are? Curled up like a shrimp! I would always ask my Nonna to make these cookies for me because I loved the cinnamon sugar on the outside which adds both crunch and sweetness.

1 cup (250 mL) butter, softened

1 cup (250 mL) sugar

3 eggs

1 tub (475 g) ricotta cheese ————

2 tsp (10 mL) vanilla

4½ cups (1.1 L) all-purpose flour (approx.)

You will need 1½ cups (375 mL) of ricotta for this recipe.

Filling

1 cup (250 mL) sugar

2 tsp (10 mL) ground cinnamon

½ cup (125 mL) butter, melted

IN A LARGE BOWL, beat butter and sugar until light and fluffy. Beat in eggs one at a time, beating well after each addition. Beat in ricotta cheese and vanilla until smooth. Gradually stir in flour 1 cup (250 mL) at a time until a stiff dough forms. Knead with hands to form smooth dough. Divide dough into 8 balls. Wrap with plastic wrap and refrigerate for about 1 hour or until firm.

Filling: Meanwhile, in a bowl stir together sugar and cinnamon.

Preheat oven to 350°F (180°C). Line baking sheets with parchment paper; set aside.

Roll out each ball into about a ¼-inch (6 mm) thin circle. Brush with some of the butter. Sprinkle with 2 Tbsp (30 mL) of the sugar mixture. Cut into 12 triangles. Roll up each triangle and form a shrimp or crescent shape. Place on baking sheet and bake in oven for about 18 minutes or until golden brown. Repeat with remaining dough.

Remove to rack and let cool completely.

MAKES 8 DOZEN COOKIES.

Place in an airtight container in the freezer for up to 3 months. They are really tasty semi-frozen when taken out of the freezer! Sometimes I can't wait for them to thaw.

Peach Cookies *Pesche Dolci*

At every bridal or wedding shower I have ever attended, these peach cookies have made an appearance. I remember seeing my aunts and other ladies at a long table helping to create the perfect rosy coloured tint for the cookie and garnishing the top with just the right amount of green licorice for the stem. When time allowed, those with piping skills would create a little green leaf with icing on top as well. I loved breaking them open to enjoy the custard inside and the soft delicate cookie that held it in its place.

4½ cups (1.1 L) all-purpose flour (approx.)
4 tsp (20 mL) baking powder
4 eggs
1½ cups (375 mL) sugar
½ cup (125 mL) 2% milk
½ cup (125 mL) canola oil
1 tsp (5 mL) lemon zest
1 tsp (5 mL) lemon juice
½ cup (125 mL) water
½ cup (125 mL brandy, anise liqueur,
  rum or sherry
Red food colouring
Half a batch of Lemon Cream (see
  recipe p. 197)

Garnish
Granulated sugar
Green string licorice
Fresh mint leaves

You can use your favourite chocolate or banana pudding filling or a simple pastry cream instead of the lemon cream.

PREHEAT OVEN TO 350°F (180°C). Line baking sheets with parchment paper; set aside.

In a large bowl, combine flour and baking powder.

In another bowl, whisk together eggs, sugar, milk, oil, lemon zest and juice. Make well in flour mixture and pour egg mixture into well. Gradually stir mixture together, taking a bit of dry ingredients each time you stir to form a soft dough. (You may need to add more flour to form the dough. If you do, add it a tablespoon at a time.)

Roll dough into 1-inch (2.5 cm) balls; place on prepared baking sheets. Have a bowl of water nearby to dampen your hands if necessary to help roll the cookie dough. Bake in oven for about 15 minutes or until lightly golden on bottom. Repeat with remaining dough. Let cool slightly.

CONTINUED NEXT PAGE >

Peach Cookies CONTINUED

While cookies are still warm, use a small paring knife to cut centres out of flat side of cookies. Leave about a ½-inch (1 cm) rim inside the cookie.

Cookies can be frozen for up to 1 week.

In a bowl, combine water, brandy and a few drops of red food colouring. The deeper the red colour the darker your peaches will be. Dip each cookie cap quickly into water mixture and set aside. When dipping the cookies into the water mixture, try to be quick about it and not let them soak in the mixture as it will soften the cookie too much and won't hold its shape. Fill each cookie half with lemon cream; place 2 halves together to form a "peach."

You can put the Lemon Cream into a piping bag and pipe into each cookie instead of spooning it in.

Roll in sugar and place in paper muffin cups on a baking sheet. Repeat with remaining cookies.

Cut licorice into short "stem" pieces; place on top end of peach with mint leaf. Place in refrigerator for at least 8 hours or until cookies have softened.

MAKES 2 DOZEN PEACHES.

You can make peaches up to 2 days ahead. They will be very soft and cake-like.

Ravioli Cookies *Biscotti Ripieni*

I have a cookie exchange each year and I like making these because they are different and have a great flavour and texture combination. You can fill them with your favourite jam, jelly or even marmalade. At my house strawberry jam still rules.

1 cup (250 mL) butter, softened	2½ cups (625 mL) all-purpose flour
⅔ cup (160 mL) sugar	¼ tsp (1 mL) baking soda
1 egg	Pinch of salt
2 tsp (10 mL) lemon zest	1 cup (250 mL) strawberry jam
2 tsp (10 mL) vanilla	(approx.)

IN A LARGE BOWL, beat butter until light. Beat in sugar and egg until smooth. Beat in zest and vanilla until well blended.

In another bowl, stir together flour, baking soda and salt. Gradually stir flour mixture into butter mixture until incorporated. Using your hands, knead the dough just long enough to form a soft dough. Divide the dough in half and wrap in plastic wrap and refrigerate for about 30 minutes or until slightly firm.

Preheat oven to 350°F (180°C). Line baking sheets with parchment paper; set aside.

Roll out half of the dough on a floured work surface into a 12 × 12-inch (30 × 30 cm) square. Cut into 32 rectangles and top each rectangle with about ½ tsp (2 mL) of the jam. Fold each rectangle to form a pocket holding the jam and use a floured fork to press edges of the pocket gently and seal. Prick the tops of each cookie.

Place cookies on prepared baking sheets and bake in oven for about 12 minutes or until edges begin to turn golden. Repeat with remaining dough.

MAKES 64 COOKIES.

Store in airtight container for up to 1 week. Cookies will soften as they sit. Freeze for up to 3 weeks.

ACKNOWLEDGEMENTS

Keeping a list of family recipes and finding lost ones is a job that I love to do, but I could not have done it without many family and friends helping. I will continue to share recipes that have been loved and enjoyed by those in my life. It is the best feeling when people taste the dishes and are reminded of their own family members who used to make these dishes for them. I hope these "Food memories" live on with generations to come.

Per La Famiglia could not have happened without many people's help, time and understanding.

Thank you to the Whitecap team who have helped along the way. Nick Rundall listened as I talked intently about my Italian heritage and family. Jordie Yow, Michelle Furbacher and Jesse Marchand made the book come to life page by page. Thank you to Moira Sanders, who helped bring cohesiveness to the book.

Jonathan Bielaski, you are an amazing photographer and I am proud to say you are a dear friend. You took the loose ideas I had in my head and brought them to life.

The days of photography I undertook could not have been completed without the help of key people who helped bake, prop style, wash dishes and help me make key decisions. Thank you Connie Raso, Donna Pitcher and Maureen Topelko for your days of help and making me laugh when I needed it most.

Thanks to my darling cousin, Sandra Buffone Maddix, you are a wordsmith and grammar expert; I appreciate and value the time you gave me for both translation and inspiration.

There was lots of food that came out of my kitchen and people who helped in deciding whether the recipe was good and as they remembered. You are all so important to me and really helped with your constructive criticism and amazing stories. Michelle, Omar, Lan, Rosa, Tom and Krishna you are wonderful friends. I have enjoyed sharing my culture with you for many years and hope to continue to for many more to come. There were also a number of my kids' friends that I had take food home to share with their families and let me know what they thought of it. I can't thank you enough for your words of encouragement and your love of Italian food.

I would like to acknowledge the work and guidance of Elizabeth Baird who sat down with me to help think out chapter ideas and what people might like in a book. She has always celebrated my love of my Italian heritage. Reading through recipes, washing dishes and rolling gnocchi are just some of the wonderful jobs she did to help these recipes become a book. Thank you Mamma Elizabeth, *ti amo*.

Thanks to James, my husband who is always there to taste another dish and enjoy a glass of wine to support my love of food. It is with him and our amazing three children—Matthew, Nicolas and Adriana—that I share these memories of many celebrations together; I can't wait for the ones still ahead. My family is the reason I love what I do and want to share it.

Without the strength and constant support of my mother and father, none of this would have ever happened. The stories and recipes would not have existed. Their guidance and love continues from generation to generation because they share it with everyone they know.

Thanks to my beautiful and talented sister Tina, her strength continues to amaze me and her determination is what I feed off of. Without her words of encouragement and constant support, trust me, many things in this book would not have come alive.

Thank you to everyone who continues to support me by coming to my cooking classes, sending emails and watching me on TV or the internet. Without your love of food and cooking I would not be able to share the delicious flavours of Italian food beyond my small circle. I appreciate being part of a bigger circle of food lovers and *amici* ("friends").

Mille grazie, Con Amore Sempre
Mangia Bene

Emily

INDEX